STEAMBOAT
LEGENDARY BUCKING HORSE

HIS LIFE & TIMES

STEAMBOAT
LEGENDARY BUCKING HORSE

AND THE COWBOYS WHO
TRIED TO TAME HIM

BY
CANDY VYVEY MOULTON
AND FLOSSIE MOULTON

HIGH PLAINS PRESS
GLENDO, WYOMING

Cover sketch by N.C. Wyeth
through Image Club Graphics.

Our thanks go to Peter Fillerup
who allowed us to use a photograph of his sculpture,
FANNING A TWISTER—STEAMBOAT,
on the cover of early printings of this book.

Library of Congress Cataloging-in-Publication Data

Moulton, Candy Vyvey, 1955-
Steamboat, legendary bucking horse : his life & times,
and the cowboys who tried to tame him /
by Candy Vyvey Moulton and Flossie Moulton.
p. cm.
Includes bibliographical references and index.
ISBN: 0-931271-18-5 (hardcover)
ISBN: 0-931271-19-3 (paper)
1. Cowboys--United States--Biography.
2. Steamboat (Horse).
3. Rodeo--Wyoming--History.
I. Moulton, Flossie, 1932-   . II. Title.
GV1833.5.m68   1992
791.8'4'0922--dc20
[B]   92-8507
CIP

HIGH PLAINS PRESS
539 CASSA ROAD
GLENDO, WYOMING 82213

This book is for all the cowboys of Wyoming,
but especially for my parents, Betty and Fox Vyvey,
who've done their share of ranchwork.
Candy Vyvey Moulton.

To the memory of my grandparents, Guy and Annie Holt,
and my mother, Gwen Holt Woodward.
Flossie Moulton.

ACKNOWLEDGMENTS

INFORMATION FOR THIS BOOK was gathered from a variety of sources including the Saratoga Historical and Cultural Association in Saratoga, Wyoming; the Grand Encampment Museum and the Encampment Public Library in Encampment, Wyoming; the University of Wyoming Coe Library, Western Heritage Center, and the Laramie Public Library in Laramie, Wyoming; the Wyoming State Archives and Old West Museum in Cheyenne, Wyoming; the Colorado History Museum in Denver, Colorado; The National Cowboy Hall of Fame in Oklahoma City, Oklahoma; and the Buffalo Bill Historical Center in Cody, Wyoming. Without the assistance and cooperation from the staffs and volunteers of those facilities our search for information related to Steamboat would not have been nearly so fruitful.

Special appreciation must go to Ann Nelson, Jean Brainerd, Shirley Flynn, Harvey Deselm, D. C. Thompson, Elva Evans, Gay Day Alcorn, Betsy Bernfeld, Emery Miller, Peter M. Fillerup, and the families of the cowboys who provided us with so much help. There are many others whom we've contacted along the way, and while we won't list them here, they must know we truly appreciate their assistance.

Finally, to our own families, Harley, Steve, Shawn, and Erin Marie, thanks for your unqualified support. Without it the story of Steamboat and his would-be conquerors would remain in the dusty pages of forgotten newspapers and historical collections.

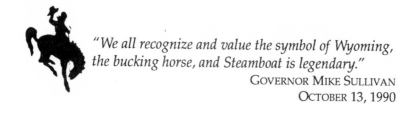

"We all recognize and value the symbol of Wyoming, the bucking horse, and Steamboat is legendary."

GOVERNOR MIKE SULLIVAN
OCTOBER 13, 1990

A LEGEND BEGINS

STEAMBOAT PRANCED INTO the dusty Laramie arena in September of 1903, his feet marking time as a dark-haired cowboy walked toward him on high-heeled boots. Both horse and man had a job to do. Outside the arena the crowd watched, knowing the Steamboat whistle was about to blow.

The horse was snubbed with a bucking rein and blindfolded with a gunny sack over his head. Even so, he was a picture of equine perfection, his black coat shiny in the afternoon sunlight.

The new World Champion Broncho Buster Guy Holt edged up to the horse, slapped his red and blue saddle blanket onto the horse's back, and felt the power as the horse tensed. The broncho saddle quickly followed the blanket, and the single cinch was pulled tight. Holt checked his boots and spurs, tightened his bandana, pulled his hat down on his head before slipping his foot into the stirrup and swinging his angora-covered leg over the horse's bunched back.

Holt was barely seated when the horse exploded into gyrations like an acrobat on a mat. Steamboat, perhaps the best bucking horse in history, bucked and jolted, turned and hopped. Holt, one of a select number of top cowboys at the turn of the century, held on for the ride of his life. He knew he was fanning a twister.

11

Swan Land and Cattle Company Two Bar Ranch Foreman Sam Moore riding Nosebag and leading Steamboat, on left, and Leopard Spots. Steamboat was first worked and ridden by cowboys on the Two Bar Ranch. (American Heritage Center, University of Wyoming.)

The story of Steamboat and his era is laced with drama, mystery, murder, and outlaws as well as cowboys, wild west shows, rodeos, and ranchers. It is pure Wyoming history—part truth, part legend. Sometimes it's difficult to tell the fact from the fiction, but the story is one of a young, wild horse who could never quite be tamed by the cowboys who tried to break him. His spirit was undaunted.

Steamboat was foaled on the Frank Foss Ranch near Chugwater, Wyoming, the offspring of a Percheron stallion and a Mexican hot blood mare. Jet black, with three white socks, and powerfully built because of his breeding, the horse proved unconquerable. He was one of several horses sold by Foss to Alexander Swan. When cowboys castrated the horse, he hit his head so hard against the ground that he broke a bone in his nose. That caused him to breathe with a whistling sound and led cowboy Jimmy Danks to give him the distinctive name, Steamboat.

The horse was first worked by cowboys on the Swan Land and Cattle Company holdings that extended across three counties from Chugwater to the upper North Platte River Valley.

Like they did to other horses rounded up in the late 1890s, cowboys out on the range worked to break the colt. Jimmy Danks is the first cowboy to ride the horse that would eventually make his mark on Wyoming history.

Danks and others tried to tame the wild cayuse, but weren't successful. The powerful horse's reputation as a bucker spread to cowboys throughout the region, and his first appearance in the rodeo arena was at the Festival of Mountain and Plain in Denver, Colorado, in 1901, with Idaho cowboy Tom Minor aboard. Over the next dozen years Steamboat pranced, cavorted, and bucked his way to fame as he pitched top riders of the day into the dirt or gave those who had the ability and perseverance necessary to stick with him the ride of their lives. Contrary to some folklore, he was ridden several times for varying lengths of time.

Steamboat's ability as a bucker might have been long forgotten, but for the fact that he was the horse depicted by the University of Wyoming on its Cowboy logo. Guy Holt is the cowboy up on Steamboat for that symbol with the 1921 design taken from a photograph made by University Professor B. C. Buffum of Holt on Steamboat at the Albany County Fair in September of 1903. That photo, showing the determination of both horse and rider, has been called by some the classic bucking horse photograph of all time.

Popular legend also names Steamboat as the bucking horse on the Wyoming license plate. Several cowboys are

The grass field at the 1903 Albany County Fair was churned by Steamboat as he tried to unseat World Champion Cowboy Guy Holt. This photo, taken by University of Wyoming Professor B.C. *Buffum, has been called the classic bucking horse photo of all time because it shows the determination of both the horse and the rider. This photo was used by the University of Wyoming in 1921 to design that institution's cowboy emblem. Some believe it also was used by artist Allen True when designing the Wyoming automobile license plate, although there is no conclusive evidence that is so. (American Heritage Center, University of Wyoming.)*

said to be the model for the automobile license, but there is no proof that artist Allen True had any particular rider in mind when he made his drawing. It's not even certain that Steamboat is the horse, though most believe that to be so, and through the years Steamboat has come to be Wyoming's legendary bucking broncho.

Cody, Wyoming, artist Peter M. Fillerup chose Steamboat as the subject for the fourteen foot sculpture placed permanently at the University of Wyoming in 1990 to commemorate the state's centennial. Steamboat's rider in the sculpture is a composite of all the early-day cowboys who mounted the famous bucking horse. With angora chaps flying and hat in hand, the cowboy of Fillerup's creation is *FANNING A TWISTER— STEAMBOAT.*

Steamboat was not the horse first used by the Wyoming National Guard to symbolize the Wyoming guardsmen in Europe during World War I. That honor went to a Sheridan horse named Red Wing and owned by George Ostrom.

But in the beginning the horse which became the symbol of Wyoming's spirit and independence was just one more long-legged foal on the range.

"I guess he thought bucking was his business."

JIMMY DANKS
IN AN ACCOUNT OF HIS FIRST RIDE ON STEAMBOAT

BORN A BUCKER

AFTER STEAMBOAT'S BIRTH in 1896, he ran the Foss range until 1899 when the Swan Land and Cattle Company purchased him along with a bunch of other horses.

When the black colt was first obtained by the Swan outfit's Two Bar Ranch, he was a three-year-old stallion. Swan cowboy Jimmy Danks told of the injury to the horse's nose that inspired the name "Steamboat": "When we throwed him to castrate him we bumpted [sic] his head and told [Two Bar Foreman] Sam Moore to look here. There was a bone in his nostril. Sam cut it out with his pocket knife. He was turned out that spring till he was four years old. Then we fetched him in to break."

Danks, the top hand on the Two Bar, and Jim Sloan were sent to the M Bar Ranch, another ranch in the Swan Company holdings, to break the new horses. It was a difficult assignment. Danks was the first man to ride the black colt in 1900 and recalled the event this way.

"We worked them colts out when we got ahold of Steamboat. Why I bitted him several times in the corral and rode him about four times in the corral. He was kind of stubborn and I would get right on to him and he would just stand there and when you screwed him a little bit with the spurs he would go to; he would buck and when he bucked he bucked hard.

And so I decided I would take him out there one day. When he come out of the corral he looked that way and this way. He blowed up at me and we had one of the damnedest saddle fights you ever saw."

Danks continued, "Sloan opened the gate and when we came out of the barn the horse looked up at me and looked this way and that, he blowed up at me and went to buckin'. He was bucking pretty hard, too hard to grab the horn, he tore me loose from there and I gave up the elbow. He went around and around. He throwed me over there and this way and that and I thought, well here I go. He went out across the field [toward] the fence and irrigation ditch. He went about one hundred yards and stopped and he didn't hit the fence or the ditch on the other side. He got along to a flat and I got along all right with him from there on. Later I said to Sloan, 'I thought you were going to haze for me,' and he said he was too busy watching the horse buck."

From that account it might be claimed that Danks is not only the first man to mount the black horse called Steamboat, but also the first man to control the horse. Danks may not have ridden Steamboat to a standstill, but at least he did not end up in the dirt.

The two cowboys moved the horses down to the Two Bar Ranch on Sybille Creek. Then the colt was taken to a range in the Goshen Hole, but there the cowboys didn't have time to work with him. Steamboat was kept with the remuda on Two Bar roundups and was in the string provided to Frank Roach, though he apparently never attempted to ride him because he'd been told by Sloan the horse was a bucker.

It's fairly clear that several of the Two Bar cowboys, whose names aren't known, attempted to ride Steamboat. Their efforts generally landed them in the dust, and the cowboys decided to keep the secret of Steamboat's bucking ability

A top hand on the Swan Land and Cattle Company's Two Bar Ranch, Jimmy Danks shows his form on an unidentified bucking horse. Danks is the first man to have mounted Steamboat and is also credited for naming the big black bucking horse. (American Heritage Center, University of Wyoming.)

to themselves. They may have figured to win some money by betting for the big black horse at roundups, where the first bucking horse contests were held.

One day in 1901, however, Duncan Clark came to visit from John Coble's Polka Dot outfit to see if the Swan Ranch had any bucking horses. The crew said Danks couldn't break Steamboat, and Clark was told he could have the horse for Coble's bucking string. Clark paid either twenty-five dollars or fifty dollars for Steamboat; records aren't clear as to the precise amount.

While he didn't like spurs and was a hard bucker, Steamboat had a smooth disposition and was not hard to halter break. He was gentle to handle and liked his oats, one of his handlers, A. S. Gillespie, wrote in the *Laramie Republican-Boomerang*. Gillespie said he could easily enter a barn stall with Steamboat, and he helped saddle him in an open field without a chute. Steamboat was perfectly formed, even though he had a large, and some said ugly, head. His big chest was evidence of the power and endurance he had when bucking.

"He would lead nice to hand; he just wanted to buck. Well he wouldn't fight you, 'til you went to riding. Kinda wanted to buck. I guess he thought bucking was his business," Danks said.

In the rodeo arena, Steamboat must have sensed that he was unequaled. Even though he usually squatted down before his first jump, he stood quietly as he was being saddled. When turned loose, Steamboat played to the crowd. He bucked fast and hard. His legs were often ramrod stiff, like pile drivers, so he jarred the cowboys to their depths. Steamboat was an entertainer, whether as a bucking horse in Denver and Cheyenne or in the arena of the Irwin Brothers Wild West Show. He was often led in parades, and Gillespie said, "Steamboat liked band music and kept step to it."

Steamboat's debut in the rodeo arena was at the Festival of Mountain and Plain in Denver in October 1901 where Tom Minor of Idaho climbed aboard, and, according to one newspaper account, stayed put until the horse stopped. Thad Sowder also mounted Steamboat that year at the Festival of Mountain and Plain.

It didn't take long for the word about Steamboat's bucking ability to get around cowboy circles. After all, many Two Bar

A raucous bunch of cowboys, headed by Hugh Clark (brother of Duncan Clark) and Marshall McPhee, race down Cheyenne's streets as part of the 1905 Frontier Days celebration. (American Heritage Center, University of Wyoming.)

hands had seen him in action on the range. Perhaps they decided it was time to let everybody in on the secret of Steamboat's power. By the following August, Steamboat was in Cheyenne for Frontier Days. Everyone associated with the broncho bucking contest knew the cowboy who drew Steamboat could win the championship if he only stuck with the big horse.

The draw went to Frank Irwin who was a small man weighing less than 120 pounds. With his brothers, Charlie and Bill, holding the horse, Frank cinched his saddle tight as Steamboat stood with feet wide apart, crouching for his first jump. As the brothers jerked away the blindfold and let the horse go, Frank's ride started like a dynamite explosion with Steamboat "sunfishing" and "swapping ends" in an attempt to unseat the wiry rider. Frank went off the right side of the horse. His foot caught in the stirrup making him a human pendulum under the horse as Steamboat bucked. Irwin eventually was thrown free, but not before being kicked by Steamboat's flying hooves.

That performance confirmed the horse's reputation, and for at least the next eight years, he was the undisputed king of the buckers. Steamboat was voted Worst Bucking Horse of the Year at the Cheyenne Frontier Days celebration in 1906 and 1907, the only years in that decade when such a designation was made. He was consistently called the "old outlaw horse" and "the worst to come off the range in many a year" by newspaper writers during that same period. Though he was a top bucker for years, old-time cowboys agree he was at the pinnacle of his career in about 1907.

"In its glory days, the Swan Company had so many brands it had to publish its own brand book so ranch hands could identify company livestock."

ARIZOLA MAGNENAT IN THE
PLATTE COUNTY RECORD-TIMES

SWAN CATTLE EMPIRE

ON THE VAST RANGE controlled by Swan Land and Cattle Company Limited, Two Bar cowboy Jimmy Danks first saddled the legendary bucking horse Steamboat. Although there is no doubt Danks was the first to ride the black horse, no clear record exists showing which other Swan cowboys might have attempted the feat.

However, many of the cowboys who did climb aboard Steamboat in the rodeo arena worked at one time or another for the Swan. It was one of the largest ranches in the West and needed top hands to gather cattle and ride the range. No doubt the cowboys attempted several times to break the horse while he was part of the Two Bar cavvy. It was their job, and Steamboat was intended to become a working cow horse even though destiny put him in the rodeo arena. Those cowboys did their jobs well, and often challenged each other in wagers to determine who were the best riders. Since Steamboat was in the horse remuda for Swan roundups on the Two Bar Ranch, it might be assumed that at times he was the horse chosen by a top hand who was determined to make the best ride.

To understand Steamboat's era, it's necessary to have some knowledge of the Swan operations which helped create both the cowboys and the legendary horse.

Wyoming was largely unsettled, a huge area of public domain, when members of the Swan family came from Iowa to seek their fortunes. The vast, grass-covered, unfenced ranges were ideal for the type of life brothers Alexander, Henry and Thomas "Black Tom" Swan were seeking, a place where cattle could roam at will, getting fat on native grasses.

The three brothers joined in partnership to operate the Swan Brothers Ranch in the Cheyenne area. The Swan brothers brought the first Hereford cattle into Wyoming Territory when they received two carloads of Hereford bulls at Cheyenne on May 14, 1878. According to an early day newspaper, the shipment was the "heaviest importation of blooded stock...ever made to the territory." In 1880 the Swan Brothers firm, which by then also included Henry's son, W. F. Swan, was dissolved.

Alexander Swan was a big man, over six feet tall, with a magnetic personality. He was public-spirited and supported a number of civic, state, cultural, and educational movements. Alex had been involved in the formation of the Wyoming Stock Growers Association, serving as president from 1876 until 1881. Swan served in the territorial legislature and, although he didn't campaign, was nearly elected to Congress in 1880, losing the election by only a twenty-five vote margin.

In quick succession, Alexander founded three businesses in Wyoming including the Swan and Frank Livestock Company on February 26, 1881; the National Cattle Company on July 16, 1881; and the Swan, Frank and Anthony Cattle Company Incorporated on August 1, 1882. The three firms were located in Carbon, Albany, and Laramie counties. Then in 1883, Swan traveled to Scotland where he successfully sold the opportunities of the American West and shares in the three businesses he represented to investors and businessmen. Alex also was hired to manage the newly-organized Swan Land

and Cattle Company Limited at a salary of ten thousand dollars per year plus expenses.

The period 1883-86 was prosperous for Alexander Swan and his Scottish investors. He initiated breeding practices to improve his cattle and continued as a member of the executive committee of the Wyoming Stock Growers Association until 1887. The Swan cattle herds included Herefords, Shorthorns and Galloways. From an initial start of fifteen thousand dollars when Alexander and Black Tom came West in 1873, the venture grew to an operation valued at fifteen million dollars.

Alex also formed the Horse Creek Land and Cattle Company, the Wyoming Hereford Association, Swan Brothers, Frank and Bernheimer, and the Ogallala Land and Cattle Company. Those were in addition to the gigantic Swan Land and Cattle Company.

By 1885 Alex was a true cattle baron who had control of more than two hundred thousand head of cattle on the western range, and he also operated a large farm at Indianola, Iowa. He fed cattle in the late fall at Grand Island, Nebraska, and at the Willow Springs Distillery in Omaha, Nebraska.

But his Scottish investors began to accuse Swan of mismanagement when it was revealed that of the 11,500 Texas steers bought in 1884 only 480 could be accounted for in 1885. On paper at least, cattle inventories were recorded at 113,625 head in 1886.

Then the swirling blizzards of 1886 and 1887 took a tremendous toll on the stock. As in past winters, the cattlemen wintered thousands of head of cattle on the open range, where the cattle primarily fended for themselves during periods of severe weather. But that winter started early with cold and snow that didn't let up. The cattlemen didn't have enough hay to feed their animals, and the herd losses were staggering.

In the spring of 1887, Alex Swan was in financial trouble. He went to the banks asking for money to tide over his operation, but was turned down. Because the Swan Land and Cattle Company had been a leader in expansion and operations in southern Wyoming, the area was startled in May 1887 when an announcement of assignment was made.

"This firm has been at the front in all cattle operations since the beginning of the great industry in Wyoming, and being practical cattlemen they have always made a success of their undertakings," the *Northwestern Live Stock Journal* reported.

"And just here we desire to go on record as saying that the assignment is not due to cattle operations, notwithstanding the great shrinkage in values for the past two years," the *Journal* further said. Rather, according to the report, Alex Swan was often too willing to "throw himself boldly into a number of large enterprises in order to help his friends out." While some of those ventures were successful a number weren't, and the drain on Swan's resources caused the problems he faced in the spring of 1887.

During his heyday Swan had run some two hundred thousand head of cattle on ranches from Scottsbluff, Nebraska, to Fort Steele, Wyoming, with holdings valued at more than fifty million dollars. After years of near phenomenal success and a wide reputation over the nation, Swan came upon hard times. In one movement of seventeen thousand head of two-year-old Texas steers, he lost 15,800 head to disease during the drive, and many of the remaining animals fell prey to weather and Indians.

Swan also was affected by the Alien Land Act of March 1887 which was passed to prevent foreigners and foreign countries from acquiring American land. Like dominoes the empire began to crumble. In May of 1887, Swan was replaced as manager of the company by Finlay Dun of Edin-burg, Scotland, who had served as secretary of the Swan Land and Cattle Company.

Even without Alex at the helm, the Swan Land and Cattle Company prospered and at one time the land holdings of the company amounted to a million acres including public lands used for grazing. In its glory days, the ranch had so many brands it was necessary to publish a brand book so foremen and ranch hands could identify the company livestock. By 1912, the Swan Land and Cattle Company Limited had thirty-two separate ranches, among them the Diamond, Kelly, M Bar, and Two Bar.

Even though he was no longer the manager, Alex Swan continued to be involved in the company after he went to Scotland and obtained forty-six thousand dollars in borrowed money without the need to put up security.

The Swan family empire was made even more extensive by several of Alexander Swan's relatives. Four of Swan's cousins were in Wyoming, establishing Swan, Wyoming, and helping extend the Swan legend.

The Pennsylvania cousins, Thomas J., called "Red Tom," Lewis, William and Obadiah, trailed Texas Longhorns into Wyoming through North Park, Colorado, in 1880, and settled the Tomahawk Ranch along the Encampment River. The Swan post office was established there June 27, 1881. They ran up to ten thousand head of cattle from 1882 to 1886.

During the tough winter of 1886, the Encampment Swans lost a lot of cattle, and reportedly said, "The only thing that the country was good for was buffalo and Indians and they both knew enough to leave in the winter." The four brothers sold their land. But before they left, they lent their name to a community that was really only a post office delivery point on the Encampment River. The town of Swan is now just another ghost in the upper North Platte valley. It is located downstream from the present-day town of Riverside, Wyoming.

Alexander's nephew, W.F. Swan, had in 1881 purchased a trail herd of Oregon cattle. He took possession at Rock Creek and altered the L road brand by reversing the iron and rebranding to make an L7.

Then W.F. bought the Hat Ranch from Carbon County Sheriff William Hawley in 1882 for thirty thousand dollars, establishing a headquarters in the North Platte Valley on Pass Creek at the base of Elk Mountain. The purchases started a pattern for W.F. and within a year he was listed as one of Carbon County's cattle kings. He expanded into the Little Snake River Valley with the purchase of the George Baggs ranches. In 1883 W.F. filed articles of incorporation for that property under the name Snake River Cattle Company, but in reality the activities were always under the auspices of the Ell Seven Cattle Company which had been founded that fall with a capital stock of one million dollars.

After the hard winter of 1886-87, W. F. Swan sold the Platte River properties and moved to the Little Snake River where the winter hadn't been so tough. But the winter of 1889-90 once again wreaked havoc with the cattle and that, coupled with low cattle prices, led his company to go out of business in 1894.

The Swan family made its mark on Wyoming history. Family members owned properties extending from Chugwater to Baggs and, on the dominant piece of ground, developed the Two Bar Ranch. On that ranch young men learned to ride and rope. They wrangled horses and trailed cattle across endless miles of Wyoming prairie, hills, and mountains. They were range riders, often called waddies, and could be found living alone, tending cattle on the far-flung open range, for weeks at a time.

During the roundups, the cowboys from all the ranches would gather to brand calves and sort cattle. They roped steers and demonstrated roping tricks. The waddies also challenged each other in the activity that was a true test of a cowboy's ability, riding bucking bronchos. Since Steamboat was in the Swan roundup cavvy, no doubt he was involved in the bucking contests. On that Swan range the cowboys built their reputations for honesty, hard work, and riding ability, while Steamboat began to make a name for himself as an outlaw.

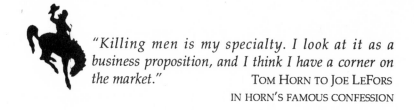

"Killing men is my specialty. I look at it as a business proposition, and I think I have a corner on the market." TOM HORN TO JOE LEFORS
IN HORN'S FAMOUS CONFESSION

RANGE MURDER AND MYSTERY

TOM HORN'S LIFE EBBED at the end of a rope in the last legal hanging held in Wyoming, and he is never known to have ridden that other renegade, Steamboat. Even so Horn's story is intertwined in unusual ways with that of the great horse.

Horn lived for periods of time at the John Coble ranch and the two were close friends. Coble also was the co-owner of Steamboat in 1901 when Horn confessed to killing fourteen-year-old Willie Nickell. Otto Plaga, who rode Steamboat at Cheyenne Frontier Days in 1905, was a key witness for the defense in Horn's trial for that killing.

Annie Holt, whose husband Guy Holt earned his reputation as a World Champion Broncho Rider atop Steamboat, recalls that Holt had slept in the same bed with Tom Horn during a round-up. Many of the letters Horn wrote while in jail awaiting his execution included references to men known to be involved with Steamboat, including Frank Stone and Duncan Clark. Those men were not just bucking horse riders and ranch hands, they were friends of Horn.

The man with whom Horn attempted to escape the Laramie County Jail on an August day prior to his death, Jim McCloud, is said to have robbed the post office in Buffalo along with Earl Shobe, who also used the aliases of Stanley Dickensen and Dick Stanley. As Dick Stanley, the cowboy

31

won the world championship on Steamboat in 1908.

Frank Stone recalled that on Horn's last ride as a free man before he was arrested for the shooting of Willie Nickell, Horn told Stone he had fifty-two notches on his gun, and the only killing he regretted was that of the Nickell boy. Stone rode Steamboat in 1902 at the Festival of Mountain and Plain in Denver.

Charlie Irwin, the eventual owner of Steamboat, and his brother Frank, who mounted the horse for Steamboat's first appearance at Cheyenne Frontier Days, sang for Horn the day he was hanged. They were among Horn's closest friends and harmonized "Life's a Railroad to Heaven" at the foot of the gallows at Horn's special request. Charlie also was given a rifle by Tom Horn that later played a role in Steamboat's story.

Horn was a key player in the final surrender of Geronimo. His work at tracking renegade Apaches was good training for his job as a detective for the Pinkerton Agency in Denver where he spent time hunting down train robbers. But the work was "too tame" for Horn, and according to his recollections, he began working in Wyoming about 1894.

Horn was originally hired as a stock detective for the Swan Land and Cattle Company, but he lived at John Coble's Iron Mountain Ranch and was eventually hired by Coble himself.

Though never proven in the courts, Horn is believed to have killed a number of men, mostly those thought to be cattle rustlers. Two of the Wyoming men Horn supposedly killed in 1895 were William Lewis, a Mill Creek rancher, and Fred Powell, a one-armed man who lived on Horse Creek.

Although Horn's name was quickly linked to the two killings, no clear or direct evidence was ever found to prove he was the gunman.

PROGRAMME
AND SOUVENIR

IRWIN BROS. CHEYENNE FRONTIER DAYS
Wild West Show

CHAS. B. IRWIN and FRANK IRWIN, Sole Owners
Permanent Address   Y6 Ranch, Cheyenne, Wyo.

Charlie and Frank Irwin, through their wild west show, played a role in the life and death of Steamboat. They were also friends of Tom Horn and sang in harmony at the hanging of the range detective. (Wyoming State Museum, Cheyenne)

In 1898 Horn's name was once again linked to shootings, this time in the Brown's Park area of Colorado where black cowboy Isom Dart and Matt Rash were gunned down. Horn was known to be in the area at the time of the killings and was injured in a saloon knifing fray a few days later in Baggs where he was almost decapitated. Little Snake River Valley residents, not knowing who he was, nursed him back to health. It wasn't until he rode north toward Rawlins that they learned the man they'd helped was Horn, the very man they had been searching for ever since Dart and Rash were killed.

Sheepman Kels Nickell ranched on Iron Mountain where he settled in 1885. Though he first raised cattle and horses, early in the 1900s he started raising the hated sheep. Cattlemen claimed the sheep, with their sharply-pointed hoofs and their close grazing habits, ruined the prairie grassland. Animosity festered between Nickell and John Coble after Nickell brought sheep into the Iron Mountain country that had been the province of cattlemen. In one altercation between the two men, Nickell stabbed Coble in the stomach.

Besides Coble, a number of other people in the area, including the cattle-raising Miller family, also held grudges against Nickell. Another stabbing incident took place in February 1901 when Jim Miller stabbed Kels Nickell.

It is here that the story takes a lethal twist as an ex-Pinkerton detective, Tom Horn, enters the scene.

It was raining and misty the morning of July 18, 1901, when Kels Nickell's fourteen-year-old son Willie started out on an errand in place of his father. Willie rode his father's horse, and as he dismounted to open a gate about a mile from his family's homestead cabin, he was shot and killed. Many thought he died from a bullet meant for his father.

Suspicion immediately fell upon the Millers because of a long-running feud between the two families. First it was

Kels Nickell homesteaded at Iron Mountain in 1885 at the mouth of a canyon. He initially raised cattle, but in about 1900 started raising sheep. That angered other area ranchers. Disagreements over the sheep and other issues escalated until on July 18, 1901, Kels Nickell's son Willie, then age 14, was killed about a mile from the homestead cabin. Range detective Tom Horn was convicted of the murder and hanged in November 1903. This view of the Nickell Ranch was drawn about 1900 by M. D. Houghton. The original oil drawing remains in the Nickell family. (Reproduction courtesy of Viola Nickell Bixler.)

thought Jim Miller, lying in wait for Kels Nickell, mistakenly shot Willie instead. Evidence also pointed to Victor Miller, Jim's son, because of past fights between him and Willie Nickell. The evidence, however, wasn't sufficient to warrant the arrest of either of the Millers.

Then attention turned to a known stock detective who worked for John Coble. When young Willie Nickell was killed, the gunman had lain in ambush, fired from a distance, and then placed a flat rock under the dead boy's head. The rock was a symbol Tom Horn used to identify his victims so his employers would know when he had completed a job and should be paid.

In 1902, Sheriff E. J. Smalley and County and Prosecuting Attorney Walter R. Stoll sought the aid of U. S. Deputy Marshal Joe LeFors to secure evidence against Horn.

During a drinking spree in Denver, Horn had boasted of killing Nickell, and LeFors joined him in another drinking bout in Cheyenne before the two men headed to the U. S. Marshal's office. It was there that Horn told LeFors he had killed Nickell. "It was the best shot I ever made and the dirtiest trick I ever done," Horn said.

Unbeknownst to Horn, another deputy and U.S. Marshal Les E. Snow, as well as stenographer Charles J. Ohnhaus, were in an adjacent room listening to the conversation—and recording the confession.

Two days later Horn was arrested at the bar of the Inter-Ocean Hotel in Cheyenne. It was on the basis of the unsigned confession that Horn was convicted and eventually hanged on November 20, 1903.

Before Horn "stretched the hemp" he captured a few more headlines.

"Horn and M'Cloud, The Daring Desperados, Break Jail" a special edition of the *Wyoming Tribune* blared Sunday, August 9, 1903.

A few months prior to the escape, Horn had displayed curiosity about Deputy Sheriff Richard Proctor's automatic weapon and asked permission to see it and to be taught how it was used. Proctor refused the request, perhaps making a decision that saved his life and that of a merry-go-round engineer during the later escape attempt.

Many people in Cheyenne responded to the fire alarm bell when Horn and Jim McCloud, both inmates at the Laramie County Jail, overpowered Proctor. The deputy put up a good fight and fired several shots in an effort to control the two inmates before the prisoners beat him and Horn took his gun. The condemned man turned the gun on Proctor and pulled the trigger. It didn't fire because the deputy had wisely flipped the safety catch just before Horn got the gun, the newspaper reported.

When the two broke out of jail, Horn went east and McCloud headed west. Horn was caught at the corner of Capitol Avenue and Twentieth Street by O. M. Eldrich, a merry-go-round engineer who engaged in a desperate running fight with the convicted murderer.

Eldrich fired shots at Horn, but Horn, though armed, never returned fire. After being grazed by one of Eldrich's bullets, Horn gave himself up. It was only after deputies arrived that Eldrich discovered the identity of the man he had chased.

McCloud was captured in a barn located within two blocks of the jail. He was badly frightened, fearing he would be shot as he surrendered, and he begged the officers to take him back to his cell as soon as possible.

Horn, meanwhile, also feared a lynching. Kels Nickell was in Cheyenne at the time of the escape and "began in a very loud voice to criticize the way the jail discipline was conducted and made a number of inflammatory speeches, attracting crowds around him, which were repeatedly ordered to disperse."

The confession which led to Horn's conviction, according to John Coble and to schoolteacher Glendolene Kimmell— who considered herself Horn's girlfriend, was obtained when Horn was extremely drunk. On such occasions the man was known to boast about his exploits and even to make up stories to awe his listener. Kimmell said the confession wasn't Horn's because it was laced with profanity, and something the range detective didn't do was cuss.

Kimmell and Coble also said "yellow journalism" practiced by the Cheyenne and Denver newspapers did as much to convict Horn as the "confession."

Although Horn was dead, his cowboy acquaintances and the rifle he had given Charlie Irwin remained to play important parts in the life of Steamboat.

"I am convinced, and I reassert it to be true, that Tom Horn was guiltless of the crime for which he died."
JOHN COBLE, IN *THE SAGA OF TOM HORN*

"When he rode a horse in front of a packed grandstand he could send a crowd into a frenzy of cheers by simply waving his hat."
WYOMING TRIBUNE ON CHARLIE IRWIN

CATTLE AND RODEO KINGS

TWO MEN FIGURE PROMINENTLY in Steamboat's rise to fame. John Coble bought the big black outlaw horse for his rodeo bucking string and owned him from 1901 until 1903. Charlie Irwin obtained Steamboat in 1903 for his rodeo bucking string and, in 1912, built a wild west show around the famous bucker.

JOHN COBLE

THE MAN WHO OBTAINED Steamboat and put him into the rodeo arena was John Cuthbert Coble, a prominent rancher in southern Wyoming who is most remembered not for his association with Steamboat, but for his connection to Tom Horn, as detailed in the preceding chapter.

Coble was born in Carlisle, Pennsylvania, and received a liberal education at Chamburg Academy, Dickinson College, and Duff's Business College in Pittsburgh, Pennsylvania, before coming West in 1877.

Coble first raised cattle in Nebraska, then moved into the Powder River country in Wyoming's Johnson County where he was engaged in ranching until 1887 when he started ranching in the Iron Mountain country between Cheyenne, Chugwater, and Bosler. Iron Mountain was also the name of a post office. The mountain, the post office, the railroad station, and

When Steamboat first entered the rodeo arena at the Festival of Mountain and Plain in Denver in 1901, he was owned by John Coble, but C.B. Irwin worked for Coble as a handler. This undated photo shows Irwin with the famed bucking horse. While Steamboat was a hard bucker, he was not a "wild horse" and was easy to handle. (American Heritage Center, University of Wyoming.)

the geographic area all took their names from the fact that iron ore was found in the vicinity in the late 1800s. Coble was highly respected by other cattlemen and belonged to the prestigious Cheyenne Club. However, he was suspended after he showed his dislike for a painting by Dutch artist Paul

Potter titled "A Bull and Cow" which hung over the bar. Coble shot holes in the leg of the bull with his forty-five caliber gun and, after his suspension, he resigned from the club.

Coble was a partner in the Iron Mountain Ranch Company, along with Frank C. Bosler. They purchased the Whitaker Ranch in the vicinity of Bosler on the Laramie Plains near Iron Mountain in 1900. Coble and Bosler remained in partnership for three years, then Coble sold his interest and left the area. While ranching with Bosler, Coble also had a string of bucking horses which he took to rodeos in the region. Steamboat was purchased for that string in 1901 marking the horse's entrance into the rodeo life.

Coble conducted experiments in the raising of fine breeds of cattle and horses. He was particularly interested in raising thoroughbred stallions. Although Coble was prominent and wealthy during the time of his association with the Iron Mountain Ranch Company, he spent most of his resources on Tom Horn's defense and his reputation suffered. Many believed that Coble was the "pay-off man" in the death of Nickell. His daughters once said the legal talent cost their father twenty-five thousand dollars. Always, they said, Coble insisted Horn was innocent of the crime. After the hanging of Horn, Coble moved to Pinedale, Wyoming, where he tried ranching on his own account. Later he went to Texas. He moved to Nevada in June of 1914 but failed to make a go of it there. He then wrote to Bosler asking for employment and threatening suicide if his request was not granted.

Despondency over financial affairs prompted Coble to shoot himself while in the lobby of the Commercial Hotel at Elko, Nevada, in 1914. Before ending his life, Coble wrote the following note to his wife: "Dear Elise, believe me, I am yours to the end, lovingly."

CHARLES IRWIN

RANCHER, STEER ROPER, wild west show promoter, rodeo man—all are titles held by Charles Burton Irwin. He helped produce Cheyenne Frontier Days rodeos during the first decade of the twentieth century. Steamboat was a part of Irwin's string of bucking horses after he bought him in 1903. When C.B. and his brother Frank formed a wild west show in 1912, their star horse was Steamboat.

A big man weighing nearly five hundred pounds in his later years, C. B., as he was known, is given much of the credit for rodeo's phenomenal growth in popularity during the time he was the king-pin of the business.

His friends included Presidents William Howard Taft and Teddy Roosevelt, for whom he named top bucking horses, General John J. Pershing, Sioux Chief Red Cloud, Charles Russell, Will Rogers, and Douglas Fairbanks, as well as the notorious Tom Horn.

From his first competition in the Cheyenne Frontier Days rodeo in 1900, C.B. was an active participant in rodeo the rest of his life. He was inducted into the Cowboy Hall of Fame in Oklahoma City in 1975.

Irwin was born in Chillicothe, Missouri, in 1875, and as a young man followed in his father's footsteps as a blacksmith. In the 1890s the Irwin family moved to Colorado Springs and set up a blacksmith shop.

In 1900 C. B. and his family moved to southeastern Wyoming where he found work with the Warren Livestock Company. At that time he was a powerful and athletic man, six feet, four inches tall and weighing about two hundred

Right: Charles Burton Irwin was a rancher, rodeo stock contractor, and a wild west show producer who owned Steamboat the better part of the horse's life. (Wyoming State Museum, Cheyenne.)

CHARLIE
IRWIN

pounds. In later years he became a giant of a man, not only in respect to his deeds, but also in his stature.

By 1901 Irwin had purchased land on Horse Creek near Cheyenne and built a homeplace that was to one day total twenty-three thousand acres and be known as the Y6.

In 1901 Irwin started working for John Coble at Bosler and took Coble's string of bucking horses down to the Festival of Mountain and Plain in Denver. Among that string was a shiny black colt called Steamboat. For the rest of Steamboat's life and the entire rodeo arena career of the famous bucker, C. B. Irwin was involved in his story. C. B. helped with Coble's rodeo string and, therefore, was associated with Steamboat as a handler until 1903 when Coble's ranch was sold and as a joke Coble gave Steamboat to the Cheyenne Elks' Lodge. The club members soon found the horse was a bucking horse with no practical value for them. Irwin bought the horse then and owned him for the rest of Steamboat's life.

By 1905 Irwin was working for the Union Pacific Railroad as a livestock agent, although later he became the line's general agent. Also in about 1905, he became plagued with a thyroid disorder that caused him to rapidly gain weight. He soon tipped the scales at 350 pounds and eventually weighed five hundred pounds.

His size didn't keep him away from horses. As a Union Pacific agent, Irwin had a specially equipped express car ready to be loaded with a posse and fast horses, should word be received of a train robbery. In fact, Irwin often joined in the chase and was instrumental in the capture of Bill Carlisle, the last of the train robbers.

C. B. also was active in rodeo circles as a stock contractor and competitor. In 1903 he "roped his steer with a very neat, business like throw" to take third place, and in 1906 Irwin was named World Champion Steer Roper.

When the Cheyenne Frontier Park moved to its present location in 1908, C. B. built his own corrals, cookhouse, and barn adjacent to the arena. He was elected to the Wyoming Fair Board and represented Cheyenne Frontier Days at the National Convention of Fair Boards.

Irwin provided stock for some of the top rodeos of the day including Cheyenne Frontier Days, the Pendleton Round-up, and the Calgary Stampede. It's likely Steamboat was used at all three rodeos, since the black horse was a regular in Irwin's bucking horse string. Cowboys are known to have ridden Steamboat in Douglas and Rawlins, indicating Irwin probably took his bucking horses to rodeos throughout Wyoming.

In 1912 C. B. and Frank Irwin formed the Irwin Brothers Wild West Show using their own stock and riders. Among the horses used for the show were Steamboat and Teddy Roosevelt, one of the other well-known bucking horses of the era.

While Steamboat was known for his twisting motion and power, Teddy Roosevelt was known for his spinning action. The two veteran horses were billed as the last featured act of the wild west show.

Irwin would advertise a twenty-five dollar prize to anyone in the crowd who could ride either Steamboat or Teddy Roosevelt. Anyone who crawled through the ropes was eligible. "One day a man did walk out of the crowd and mounted Teddy Roosevelt and by getting one hand full of saddle strings behind the saddle and the horn in the other he managed to stay aboard and get the $25 offered," a newspaper account said.

If no one accepted Irwin's challenge, one of his men would ride the horses. That is generally what happened.

Irwin provided stock for use at Cheyenne Frontier Days until 1913 when Eddie McCarty and Van Guilford got the contract to furnish stock for the Cheyenne show. The change meant Steamboat no longer performed during Frontier Days because he was in Irwin's bucking string.

But Steamboat wasn't put out to pasture since Irwin's Wild West Show was on the road throughout the West in 1913 and 1914. The show went to such places as San Francisco, Los Angeles, and Riverside, California, Reno and Las Vegas, Nevada, towns in Oregon and Idaho, Salt Lake City and Ogden, Utah, and Evanston and Laramie, Wyoming.

C.B.'s son, Floyd and daughters Joella, Pauline, and Frances, were all top hands who starred in the Irwin Brothers Wild West Show. Floyd, a broncho rider, crack steer roper, trick rider, trick roper, and relay rider was killed at the opening day of Cheyenne Frontier Days in 1917. His death led C.B. to disband the Wild West Show, although he continued as a rodeo livestock contractor.

Following World War I, C.B. became interested in thoroughbred horse racing, and, by 1923, he was the nation's leading trainer setting a phenomenal record of 147 wins.

Irwin continued to ranch near Meridan, Wyoming, and was going to Cheyenne from the Y6 in March of 1934 when the automobile he was riding in, driven by his son-in-law Claude Sawyer, blew a front tire and overturned in a ditch, killing Irwin.

Irwin's funeral was attended by about twelve hundred of his friends with a quartet singing four songs including "The Last Roundup."

Writer Will Rogers, who had been a good friend of Irwin, wrote, "That other world up there is going to hear a whoop at the gate and a yell saying 'Saint Peter, open up that main gate, for there is a real cowboy coming into the old home ranch. I am riding old Steamboat bareback and using Teddy Roosevelt for a pack horse. From now on this outfit is going to be wild, for I never worked with a tame one.'"

"These people are real cowboys and real cowgirls, born and reared on the open range."

FROM AN
IRWIN BROTHERS WILD WEST SHOW PROGRAM

THE WILD WEST

LONG BEFORE STEAMBOAT and the Irwin Brothers teamed up to hit the road with the Irwin Brothers Wild West Show people were enamored with the West. Maybe as a result of that, the phenomena called the Wild West Show began to take root in the minds of men such as William F. Cody, better known to the world as Buffalo Bill, Gordon Lillie well-known as Pawnee Bill, and a number of others over a period of years. The Irwin Brothers Wild West Show started in 1912 at a time when many shows were in a decline.

The word "circus" was anathema on the Buffalo Bill lot. So was the word "show" or "exhibition." From 1885 until 1930, there were at least 115 wild west shows, ranging from the large shows to very small ones, including the "concerts" after shows and other combinations with circuses.

Before the time of the wild west show the cowboy was no hero. President Chester A. Arthur in his 1881 message to Congress denounced a band of "armed desperadoes known as cowboys" as a menace to the peace of Arizona. The same president Arthur was threatened with kidnapping by a party of cowboys during a trip west in 1883. The working cowboys had little glamour in their lives. They spent much of their time on lonely rides gathering cattle. Buffalo Bill not only helped the cowboy hero along his way, he also, surprisingly, changed

47

the common man's concept of Indians. He employed mainly Sioux who rode horses and wore feathered headdresses.

In 1882 Buffalo Bill had planned North's Platte's "Old Glory Blow Out." Some doubted his abilities to do it. He proposed a demonstration of his methods of killing buffalo, using steers and blank ammunition. He even knew where he might borrow a small herd of privately-owned buffalo. Cody persuaded businessmen to offer prizes for roping, shooting, riding, and broncho breaking events. Five thousand handbills were sent out.

Cody hoped for one hundred cowboys; one thousand showed up to participate. The unprecedented and unexpected success gave Cody an idea. Buffalo Bill announced his intention of organizing a cowboy exhibit and using the name Wild West Show.

Buffalo Bill had been pursuing a theatrical career, and he continued that during the winter of 1882-83, but he also signed talent and sought properties for the wild west show.

The first rehearsal of the show was at Colville (later Columbus), Nebraska. A runaway Deadwood Stagecoach which was drawn by a team of almost unbroken mules nearly caused a disaster. Major Frank North suggested that what they needed was more illusion and less realism, some worn out, hack horses, and old Indians with less ambition.

The first time the Buffalo Bill Wild West Show took to the road for a tour of the United States was in 1884. A deal had been made with James A. Bailey of Barnum and Bailey to provide transportation.

In 1889 Buffalo Bill took his show to Europe for the first time. The Shah of Persia, Nasr-ul-Deen, attended, and Queen Isabella of Spain rode in the Deadwood Stagecoach. The 1891 tour went through Germany, and the 1892 season opened with a return to Earl's Court in London. There Buffalo

Bill met Queen Victoria, who commanded a performance on the lawn and tennis grounds at Windsor Castle. No one had been allowed to perform there since the death of her Prince Consort some years earlier.

It is sometimes difficult to understand how these huge and expensive aggregations could make a profit from audiences at fifty cents a head. Of course many failed, but in places throngs of people attended. In one audience 41,448 were counted. In five weeks at Gloucester Beach, New Jersey, 150,000 people saw the Pawnee Bill Show.

Some wild west show producers liked to claim that rodeo was spawned from their shows. It is generally accepted, though, that rodeo began in the corrals or on the range of the many ranches where cowboys in their spare time pitted their skills against horses in the ranch remuda and against each other. Those horses who resisted bit and saddle were their greatest challenge and entertainment, and that is how many rodeo bucking horses, including Steamboat, got their starts.

Rodeo performances, however, are derived in part from the wild west show; the difference is that rodeo is a competitive sport. A traveling rodeo of hired contestants who rode exhibition rides for a salary might fit the definition of the wild west show.

It is difficult to determine which of the cowboys who were involved with Steamboat also rode with the Buffalo Bill show. Those known to have signed on to travel with Buffalo Bill were William "Pecos" Craver, Art Acord, Harry Webb, Thad Sowder, Fred Dodge, Cravel Pagus, and Harry Brennan. It can be assumed that any one of the men known to have ridden Steamboat, as the best bucking horse riders in the world at that time, could have ridden in the Buffalo Bill show when the show was presented close to their homes. Guy Holt of Hecla, Wyoming, took his wife and two young daughters on

OLD STEAMBOAT

Worst Outlaw in the World--The Horse Which Threw the Best of Them

IRWIN BROS. CHEYENNE Frontier Days **WILD WEST SHOW**

Perhaps the only wild west show to feature a horse as the star was the Irwin Brothers Wild West Show highlighting Old Steamboat. The back of this program pictured Steamboat while the front was devoted to top cowboys and cowgirls. (Wyoming State Museum, Cheyenne.)

the train to North Platte, Nebraska, in 1908, for an appearance with the show.

Many of those men who had success riding Steamboat were associated with the Irwin Brothers show because Steamboat was a regular bucking horse for that company.

Buffalo Bill also showed interest in Steamboat. Some stories say he offered two thousand dollars for the black horse, but when he sent one of his men, Cravel Pagus, to Laramie to try to ride him, the man was unseated and Buffalo Bill lost interest in the horse.

Buffalo Bill made a farewell speech in Madison Square Garden in 1910 after his show had grossed a million dollars, but even so he extended his series of farewell exhibitions through 1910 and 1911. As profits slid, the Buffalo Bill and Pawnee Bill shows faltered, and after much legal maneuvering, the shows were sold at auction in September 1913.

The Irwin Brothers Wild West Show was formed in 1912, but the company had been in existence as early as 1902, though by different names. Most references to the Irwin operation from 1902 to 1910 were as a bucking string owned by C. B. However, he also had other acts on occasion and often billed the outfit as the Irwin Brothers Cheyenne Frontier Days Wild West Show.

In fact he used the term Cheyenne Frontier Days in connection with his show so often that finally in 1913 the Cheyenne Frontier Days committee went to court for an injunction prohibiting Irwin from using that term in association with his wild west show.

C. B. was associated with Charlie Hirsig in 1910, and the two took the wild west show they had put together to the West Coast where they promoted Steamboat and won money in wagers when various cowboys or their backers bet a skilled rider could ride Steamboat to a standstill. One of those wagers involved Art Acord, a top hand, who, however, was unsuccessful in his attempt on Steamboat.

Always the wager included the stipulation that the rider had to whip and scratch the horse as the ride was made. Irwin and Hirsig knew Steamboat wouldn't stand for either a quirt or spurs upon his hide.

The Irwin Brothers troop included many of the performers who originally worked for Buffalo Bill, but it was primarily a family affair with the stars including Frank Irwin and the children of C. B. Irwin—Floyd, Joella, Frances, and Pauline. Other regulars with the show were Bill Irwin's daughter, Gladys, his son, Sharkey, and his wife, Margaret.

The list of honors held by those regular performers is impressive. C. B. Irwin was World Champion Steer Roper in 1906, Frank Irwin was a winner of the men's relay race and the wild horse race numerous times at Cheyenne Frontier Days, Margaret Irwin won the ladies' relay race twice and was the All Around Cowgirl of 1902, 1903, and 1904 at Cheyenne Frontier Days, Floyd Irwin was a champion trick roper and rider, Joella Irwin and Pauline Irwin each won the ladies' championship twice, and Gladys Irwin was defeated only by her cousins.

Others performing with the Irwin Brothers included two-time world champion broncho buster Clayton Danks and his wife, Marie, a world champion relay rider. The show also featured Sioux Indians from the Pine Ridge Agency in South Dakota, the Al Fairbrothers Band from Omaha, Nebraska, and "all the cowboys in Wyoming who were any good," according to Gladys Irwin Foster in an article in the *Wyoming Eagle* in 1970.

The Irwin Brothers Show was performed throughout North America—from New York City to San Francisco and from Winnipeg to El Paso. Performances were given for

Presidents Theodore Roosevelt and William Howard Taft with bucking horses named for each man.

Stationery for the show had endorsements from some of those who saw it, including Roosevelt ("Saw the show twice in 1904 and 1912—best in the world"), Taft ("Nothing like it; worth going miles to witness") and U. S. Senator Francis E. Warren ("Best show on earth").

A. R. Cory of the Iowa State Fair in Des Moines said the show broke attendance records in 1912 and added that the cowboys and cowgirls were the real thing. W. R. Miller, secretary of the Nebraska State Fair, said gate receipts there in 1912 were the biggest ever.

Like other wild west shows of the era, the Irwin Brothers traveled from one performance to the next by train. One advertisement noted the company traveled in "plush railroad cars."

Moving the show itself would have been quite an undertaking. A contract between Irwin Brothers and the Spokane Interstate Fair in 1914 noted the Irwin Brothers would deliver twenty carloads of livestock and show paraphernalia for a performance including at least 125 head of livestock and one hundred people.

The Spokane organizers agreed to pay sixty-two hundred dollars for the performance and also to pay all the cash received from the night gate and grandstand receipts in excess of fifteen thousand dollars and fifty percent of all receipts collected over twenty thousand dollars.

One full page newspaper advertisement about the show outlined the performers including the following bucking horses: Old Steamboat, Teddy Roosevelt, Aeroplane, Senator Warren, Young Steamboat, Silver City, Whizzer, Biplane, Nevada Kid, Bill Taft, Archbishop, Wildcat, Gin Fizz, Cheyenne Red Bird, Laramie Plains Red Bird, Red Sandy, Miller's Kid, Hot Shot, Woodrow Wilson, and War Paint.

The Irwin Brothers Wild West Show was in operation and on the road from 1912 until 1917; then tragedy struck. On the opening day of Cheyenne Frontier Days that year, Floyd Irwin, C.B.'s son and the arena director for the wild west show, was killed in a steer roping accident. C.B., like the true businessman that he was, continued through the Frontier Days celebration, assisting with the program and working with the stock. But after all the races were run and all the rides were made, C.B. stood at the edge of the abandoned Frontier ground, his large body shaking with grief over the death of his only son.

Although C.B. continued as a rodeo stock contractor, following Floyd's death the Irwin Brothers Wild West Show was disbanded.

The wild west show in its beginning was a representation of an historical era that was still contemporary. As time went on, dramatization continued the illusion, as did the accompanying popular literature. The pulp magazine writers of the day glorified almost everything the cowboy did, and, if in trying to live up to the legend, cowboys reached a little high for a share of immortality, it was only because they thought that they deserved it. Perhaps they did.

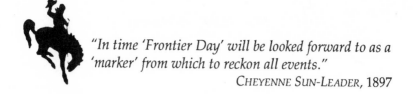

KING OF THE
HURRICANE DECK

Steamboat's first rodeo performance was in Denver at the Festival of Mountain and Plain, but his reputation was made in the Cheyenne arena at Frontier Days.

The Cheyenne celebration started in 1897 upon the suggestion of Union Pacific Railroad passenger agent F. W. Angier and *Cheyenne Daily Sun-Leader* editor E. A. Slack. The idea sprouted from the Greeley, Colorado, "Potato Day."

Slack first presented the concept of Cheyenne having its own celebration in his newspaper column. He urged citizens to get the old timers together, round up some wild horses, stagecoaches and Indians, and have a Frontier Day.

Not long after the idea became public, Cheyenne Mayor William R. Schnitger appointed a committee to organize the celebration. The group acted quickly. Slack made his suggestion for a celebration August 27, 1897, and the first Frontier Day was held less than a month later on September 23, 1897.

Special excursion trains brought visitors to the Wyoming capital city. Besides bucking contests, the Frontier committee planned a mock attack on the Deadwood Stagecoach and a mock hanging of *Laramie Boomerang* newspaper editor and humorist Bill Nye.

The 1897 Frontier Day was recalled by Ida Gilliand Fox of Cheyenne in a 1979 newspaper article. "We met Uncle

John and his family and other neighbors and all went to Cheyenne on the 4:30 A. M. train. I remember only a little of that day—how we had to stand along the railing around the race track at the old Frontier Park all afternoon, Mama grabbing Helen and running, me following, whenever a bucking horse or a steer headed our way."

Hundreds of visitors were present for the show that started with the firing of cannons by Fort D. A. Russell troops and the sound of hundreds of citizens shooting rifles, pistols, and shotguns.

"Horses jumped fences, men were knocked down, and were thought killed, but we are happy to announce that no death resulted," the press reported.

The event was strongly criticized by some newspapers as a "rough-neck show seeking to perpetuate the spirit of western rowdyism through which the West is passing."

"The influence of Frontier Day is not elevating in character. Our visitors know that the stage holdup, the vigilantes and the ox team departed years ago. And it is a curious and inexplicable thing, the unaccountable desire of dozens of ladies to stand in the race track totally oblivious to the extreme novelty and danger of their position, and while it was a relief to see them grab their petticoats and get away safely from the deadly feet of the wild and crazy horses, the spectacle was not edifying and should be dispensed with next year," another paper reported.

The Cheyenne organizers didn't heed the suggestion of the press, and Frontier Day was soon expanded into a multi-day event that included parades, cowboy contests and races, Indians and stagecoach holdups. The broncho riding was always a major attraction. The cowboys who participated spent their lives on the range working cattle. They usually worked the semi-annual range roundups with their outfits. In the evenings, after their regular work was done, the cowboys pitted their skills against each other. So when the event started they had an opportunity to display their talents to the crowds that assembled in Cheyenne.

Often when they got to Frontier Days the cowboys were backed by the owners of the ranches for which they worked; the contest was one of man against horse, and also a chance for ranchers to see who employed the best cowboys.

In tradition of contests of the times, the cowboys at Frontier Days rode with saddles. To make a qualified ride, a cowboy had to stay aboard his horse until it came to a standstill. The rider wasn't allowed to "pull leather" or grab any portion of the saddle, but he was allowed to fan the horse with a hat, to whip it with a rawhide quirt, and usually to spur the horse.

Cowboys weren't required to spur the horse, and in the case of Steamboat they seldom did. The black bucker hated spurs, and also the cowboys had to keep all their wits and efforts concentrated on staying aboard.

The cowboys used spurs from the time Frontier Days started until 1907 when the judges declared it would be a better contest if no spurs were used. While some cowboys spurred to make their horse buck harder, many used them to grip the side of their mounts, and therefore, stay in the saddle until the horse quit bucking. Without spurs, the horse had a better chance of throwing the rider. Often the use of spurs was part of a wager cowboys made with each other. Jake Maring and Sam Scoville, in 1905, both had bets that they could ride Steamboat and spur him, too. Though Maring lost the wager, Scoville apparently was successful.

"Scoville rode the outlaw to a standstill, quirting him every jump and incidentally won a side bet of $100 that he would scratch the animal during his ride," the *Wyoming Semi-Weekly Tribune* reported on September 8, 1905.

Spurs were used again at Frontier Days in 1908, but in 1909 the Wyoming Humane Society ruled they couldn't be used. The cowboys went by the ruling that year and the next, but had their spurs back on their boots in 1911.

Definite rules for the rodeo events started developing in 1905. Judges and contestants agreed the winner should be based upon averages, rather than on the best ride on one bucking horse or the fastest time for one performance.

Often the horses used in the rodeos were brought to the event by the cowboys themselves; they were range horses rounded up on the prairie. They had strength and stamina due to their mustang breeding. The early-day horses were not trained buckers, but generally were horses born and raised in the grass country of Wyoming found to be unbreakable and difficult to handle by anyone except the most expert horseman.

Because the horses saw little use they generally were strong and powerful, although often they also were vicious and dangerous and would attempt to kick or strike a rider thrown from the saddle.

During his era, Steamboat was unequaled in his fury when a rider climbed aboard. Although many top cowboys challenged Steamboat's hurricane deck, only a very few managed to ride him successfully. Riding Steamboat was not at all like riding one of today's bucking horses because to make a productive ride the cowboy had to stay aboard the horse until it came to a standstill; there was no such thing as an eight-second rule.

There were no chutes, so horses were led to the middle of the arena and saddled in the open. That process took lots of time, but the spectators didn't mind. They felt it was a part of the show. Generally the horses were blindfolded or "eared down" while cowboys tightened their riggings. Steamboat was seldom "eared down" because he stood quietly while being saddled. However, on at least one occasion, Steamboat started bucking before the blindfold was completely removed, making a wild ride for the cowboy aboard. It was an unwritten rule of the arena that a cowboy saddled his own mount. That way if something went wrong with the rigging during the ride, he had nobody to blame but himself.

After saddling the outlaw, a cowboy lightly stepped aboard and the horse was turned loose. There was no time to measure the hack rein before the hurricane deck of a wild broncho started to pitch. The cowboys of that era used a different bucking rein than modern cowboys do. At the turn of the century bucking horses wore hackamores with double reins. Many cowboys rode holding onto the reins with both hands, one on either side of the horse.

While Frontier Days named a champion broncho buster every year, it sometimes also selected the Worst Bucking Horse of the Year, and newspaper accounts of the rodeos from 1900 to 1915 gave as much play to the horses as they did to the riders.

During his bucking career, Steamboat was chosen as the Worst Bucking Horse of the Year at Frontier Days in 1907 and 1908, and reporters often dubbed him the "Outlaw Horse" or "the worst to come off the range in many a year." The title of Worst Bucking Horse was as coveted as that of World Champion Broncho Rider. For C. B. Irwin, who owned Steamboat during most of his rodeo career, the title meant people would not only come to Frontier Days to see the horse but also attend the Irwin Brothers Wild West Show featuring Steamboat.

Few cowboys who went on to win the World Championship did so by riding Steamboat in either a preliminary or final round competition. That is because the horse was so powerful and successful at dumping riders that the best riders often were disqualified on Steamboat, when they would have won the championship had they drawn a different mount.

Some were successful in riding the horse and winning the title though, including Harry Brennan, who rode Steamboat in the preliminaries in 1905 when he was crowned champion; Dick Stanley, who won on him in 1908; and Clayton Danks, who claimed the honor atop Steamboat in 1909.

Others weren't as successful, including Billy Murray who lost his chance at a world championship in 1906 when he was in the lead for the title. Murray was in a three-way ride-off with William Grieser and Clayton Danks when he drew Steamboat. The outlaw horse didn't let any grass grow under his feet, and Murray bit the dust. Cowboy John Dodge, who was up for the top honor against Danks in 1907, likewise lost his chance at the title.

"The bucking finals proved spectacular in the extreme," the *Wyoming Tribune* reported on July 29, 1907. "After conferring together the judges decided that the contest lay between Johnnie Dodge and Clayton Danks. The men drew lots, Danks drawing Millbrook and Dodge Old Steamboat. The latter was unfortunate, for the king of the buckers, Old Steamboat, [was] without doubt the worst bucking horse in the world, and after bucking until his rider was almost exhausted Steamboat began a new series of contortions which finally dumped his weakened rider over his head and it was simply a matter of Danks sticking to Millbrook to win the world championship."

Though the cowboys were out to see who was the best, they were a good-natured bunch, and most of them were friends, having worked together on ranches and roundups. One writer recalled an incident in 1910 involving Dick Stanley, the man who unmercifully conquered Steamboat in 1908 to win the world championship.

In 1910 Stanley mounted Rocking Chair but didn't make a clean ride. Some of the cowboys didn't care for Stanley. One said, "He owns a Wild West Show and is no longer a cow-punch, a little too good for the boys." It wasn't too surprising, then that, Hugh Clark, immediately after Stanley pulled leather, grasped a megaphone, and riding up and down the track, announced in a triumphant tone, "He pulled leather. He pulled leather."

Excursion trains from Denver brought many visitors to Wyoming's capital city. In 1903 the bleachers were full when the Denver train arrived, and there was no seating left for the Colorado visitors. "A great number of carriages lined the outer edge of the half-mile track, while every man who could beg or borrow a horse was mounted and occupied a coveted position inside the ring," the *Wyoming Tribune* reported.

At one celebration the stands were filled and the crowd ready for action when exactly that happened. The heavens burst open and a cloudburst turned the race track in front of the grandstand, where the events would take place, into a quagmire. The cowboys said it was too dangerous to ride in the deep mud and that the show should be postponed. Such an action was unthinkable to the show promoters who didn't know how to explain to the crowd.

The organizers decided to have Bertha Keppernick, a promising young woman bucking horse rider, ride a wild horse in front of the grandstand.

"This she did, one of the worst buckers I have ever seen, and she stayed on him all the time. Part of the time he was up in the air on his hind feet; once he fell backward, and the girl deftly slid to one side only to mount him again as he got up. She rode him in the mud to a finish, and the crowd went wild with enthusiasm. Result, the cowboys thought that if a girl can ride in the mud, we can too, and the show was pulled

Young Steamboat, held here by Hugh Clark, was a half-brother to the famed Steamboat. Both horses were top buckers, but Old Steamboat was the true king of the hurricane deck. (American Heritage Center, University of Wyoming.)

off," Warren Richardson, chairman of the first Frontier Days committee once recalled.

"The real active idea of Woman Suffrage was thus demonstrated in Wyoming at a Frontier Days' Celebration... Hurrah for the Wyoming gals! They lead in everything!" Richardson said.

It should be noted that two horses popular during the era went by the name Steamboat. A number of cowboys, including World Champion Guy Holt in 1903, won on a horse called Young Steamboat who was a half-brother to Old Steamboat. Though similar in conformation due to their breeding, the two horses could be easily distinguished by their feet. Old Steamboat had three white socks, two on his back feet and one on a front foot. Young Steamboat had four white socks. Both horses were black with a white forelock star, but only one was the true king of the hurricane deck, and that was Old Steamboat.

The black horse is one of five horses named by the National Cowboy Hall of Fame to the Roll of Great Bucking Horses. The other four are Midnight, Five Minutes to Midnight, Tipperary, and Hell's Angels.

Midnight was found in Canada by rodeo stock contractor Eddie McCarty and the horse lived from 1910 to 1936. McCarty also found Five Minutes to Midnight, a horse which lived from 1924 to 1947. Hell's Angels was foaled on the Lew Parks Ranch near Dillon, Montana, in 1927 out of a Percheron stallion and a pinto mare. In 1932, he entered the rodeo arena as a bucking horse, and the following year Mike Hastings bought the horse. He quickly gained a reputation as a tough bucking horse and died in 1942 on a train returning from New York. Like Steamboat, Tipperary was in the rodeo arena early in the twentieth century. He was born in 1910 and died in 1932.

During his era, Steamboat was rivaled in the Cheyenne arena by such horses as Teddy Roosevelt and Millbrook.

Steamboat was before the public at Cheyenne Frontier Days for eleven years. When Irwin lost the stock contract in 1913, Steamboat no longer appeared there. He'd performed "like an opera singer on the stage for a stated price," one writer said. "He has won hundreds of dollars for his owners each year by unseating the dare-devils who have tried to ride him. He is not as profitable as in former years, partly because people will not bet on him. Then some seem to think he has seen his best days, but do you wonder at it, fifteen years old and leading such a strenuous life."

"When Steamboat's day was over, I think a part of rodeo ended for me, too. I missed that black beneath me the way you miss a partner who has grubstaked you for years."

CLAYTON DANKS IN
FRONTIER TIMES, 1962

DARKNESS FALLS

THE LIFE OF STEAMBOAT was ended with a blast from Tom Horn's gun at Frontier Park in Cheyenne, October 14, 1914. Steamboat performed until his final days with the Irwin Brothers Wild West Show and was in Salt Lake City, Utah, with the show when he became badly cut with wire when the penned horses were frightened during a thunder and lightning storm.

Steamboat was returned to Wyoming, but blood poisoning set in, and the veterinarians declared there was no way to save the horse.

An obituary on Steamboat in the *Cheyenne Daily Leader,* October 15, 1914, told the story this way:

> Old Steamboat, the grand old horse of the passing west is dead. The horse that has nipped in the bud the fondest hopes of many a broncho buster, the horse that has sent fear into the ranks of the veteran busters is no more.
>
> Old Steamboat's demise was premeditated. It was necessitated by the suffering from blood poisoning resulting from an injury inflected [sic] recently while with the Irwin Bros.' wild west show. A bullet fired from the rifle of the notorious Tom Horn into the skull of the animal relieved further suffering and brot [sic] to a sad end one of the most notable careers ever enjoyed by a horse.

The caption under this photograph which appeared in the
Wyoming Eagle reads: STEAMBOAT, *"The meanest bucking bronc in
the world," is shown with one of the West's most famous bronc
riders, and world champion in 1907, Clayton Danks, well known
Lander resident, in this picture taken at Frontier Days in 1908.
Steamboat, docile while being handled, but dynamite when
ridden, lives in legend in Cowboy land from the Pecos country to
the Montana grasslands. The world famed horse was featured in
every major rodeo in the United States, including the Mountain
and Plain Festival in Denver and Frontier Days in Cheyenne, and
traveled with the Irwin Brothers Show on exhibition during his
last years. He was mercifully shot in 1914 in Cheyenne after
suffering a serious injury. His memory may some day be
permanently symbolized with a statue placed on Prexy's pasture
on the University of Wyoming campus, as a symbol of Wyoming
spirit. The old stereoscopic photo was lent by Mrs. L. M. Foster,
Campstool Route as a result of two articles on Steamboat
appearing in the EAGLE. (Photo 1908 by Ed Tangen)*
(American Heritage Center, University of Wyoming.)

The reminiscences of old range men are void of the story of a horse ever reared on the nutritious grasses of the Wyoming plains that was ever as vicious or that possessed the endurance and stamina found in "Old Steamboat."

Since four years after birth, Steamboat has been putting into flight and ridiculing the attempts of his would-be conquerers. Riders of fame from all over the world have sought to civilize him but their attempts proved futile. Only once did a rider succeed in remaining astride the pitching and plunging form of Old Steamboat and that rider was Dick Stanley of Portland, Ore., who was probably one of the most death-defying busters ever turned out on the range. Stanley rode Steamboat to a standstill in [1908] but the horse was handicapped and fought against odds. The turf was heavy and the horse was unable to get a foothold for his unusual feats.

Steamboat was often spoken of as the "Lord of the Plains" and proved the stellar attraction whenever exhibited at a wild west show. He participated in every Frontier celebration in this city up until 1912 and in scores elsewhere. In the past few years he has been used exclusively by the Irwin Bros.' wild west show.

He was "farmed off" to the Cheyenne Elk Lodge by John C. Coble, manager of the Bosler ranch. It was suggested that Steamboat supplant the traditional "goat," but subsequently the lodge discovered that Steamboat had its "Angora" instead. Steamboat later came into the possession of Charlie Irwin.

There was much grief attached to the execution of the old lord of the plains as he stood defiant, fire flashing from his eyes, until the fatal shot dispatched him.

The newspaper obituary of the horse is an indication of his prominence, but it is not totally accurate, since Dick Stanley probably is not the only man ever to ride Steamboat to a standstill. He is, however, the one most often credited with that feat. Also, when Coble gave Steamboat to the Elks' Lodge, he meant the horse to be the "goat" the lodge used for some of its functions. However, when the Elks Club members realized that Steamboat was really a bucking horse, they knew they'd been suckered by Coble.

It is probably a coincidence that Tom Horn's gun was fetched by Charlie Irwin when it became clear that Steamboat couldn't be saved. But the use of Horn's gun ties two legendary figures of the West together in an ironic manner.

Among those present when Steamboat was killed were Floyd Irwin, John Rick, Bob Lee, and Paul R. Hansen. Although most reports are that the mighty bucker was laid to rest where he had pitched so many top cowboys into the dirt and mud—at Frontier Park in Cheyenne—Hansen in 1955 said that's not the way it was.

"Steamboat is not buried at Frontier Park," Hansen said in an interview in the *Cheyenne Tribune*, June 2, 1955. "He was buried at the old city dump where he was destroyed in 1914. A lot of people think he was buried at the park, but that story is not true."

Steamboat was injured in Salt Lake, Hansen said. "We had to load Steamboat that night and bring him back to Cheyenne.... When we got here the horse was terribly swollen and dying. The only humane thing to do was to destroy him. It was decided to do this at the city dump."

Wherever the end came for Steamboat and wherever his remains lie, one thing is certain, his spirit is at Frontier Park in Cheyenne where he thrilled crowds, dumped cowboys, and kicked his heels for a dozen years.

"Steamboat left a fine heritage of the art of bucking, in his prime he was without peer in the art of cracking off riders."

A.S. "BUD " GILLESPIE AND R. H. "BOB" BURNS IN
STEAMBOAT SYMBOL OF WYOMING SPIRIT, 1952

GONE BUT
NOT FORGOTTEN

It's an old and on-going argument as to which bronc, which rider, and which photograph inspired the bucking horse that is depicted on the Wyoming license plates. This silhouetted rider has become a symbol of Wyoming better known than any other emblem. The official story and position is that the silhouette is an artist's conception drawn by Allen True of Denver, not intended to represent any individual horse or rider.

Different geographic areas of Wyoming tend to have their regional favorites as to which cowboy the emblem was patterned after, if indeed it was a real cowboy the artist had in mind.

There is little argument, however, that the horse is Steamboat. Even if True didn't have the black bucking horse in mind when he designed the plate, by association through the years the license silhouette has become that of Steamboat.

According to various accounts—from family folklore to published records, the cowboy is Jake Maring, Guy Holt or Stub Farlow. In the Laramie area, it is believed by some that Jake Maring is the rider on the license plate. The story is that in 1936, then-Secretary of State Lester C. Hunt and former broncho rider Jake Maring were in a conversation at the Laramie Elks' Club. Hunt promised Maring that when he was elected Governor of Wyoming he would see that Maring's picture was placed on the Wyoming license plates. Hunt did put the bucking horse on the license plates in 1936. The two men had a disagreement prior to that however, and Governor Hunt refused to identify the cowboy.

According to an account by Hunt of the license plate design, "Many stories have appeared in the press—their origin, I don't know—saying that the bucking horse license plate was a certain horse and the rider was Mr. Farlow. Such is not the case, but I did have 'Stub' Farlow in mind when designing the plate." Stub Farlow was a contemporary of Jake Maring and was from the Lander area.

Hunt wanted to put a bucking horse and cowboy on the Wyoming license plate to symbolize the cowboy state and said he had Farlow in mind because he was the "most typical cowboy that it was my pleasure to know."

Hunt contacted Denver artist Allen True who painted the murals in the House and Senate Chambers at the Wyoming State Capitol in Cheyenne. "I contacted Mr. True by telephone and asked him if he would mind coming to Wyoming, which he did one Sunday morning and I explained to him in detail what I had in mind. Mr. True said he would be glad to make such a drawing. Mr. True was paid $75 for the drawing," Hunt said.

"[I] have in the intervening years, been pleased that I had Mr. True do the drawing rather than use a photograph of a bucking horse, in that Mr. True, through his knowledge of art, understood what design could be stamped out in steel and retain its identity at some distance. He therefore made the drawing with only one bridle rein, and only one front left foot on the horse and with only one rider's foot."

Upon the drawing's completion a copyright was obtained so others can't use the truly unique design. That copyright

ORIGINAL DRAWING OF "BUCKING HORSE" LICENSE PLATE

Colorado artist Allen True drew the original design for the Wyoming bucking horse that has been on the state's automobile license plate since 1936. It's uncertain whether the horse and rider in the drawing are modeled after actual figures. (Wyoming State Museum.)

caused controversy on its own because Hunt obtained it in his name and not the name of the State of Wyoming. In later years, the copyright was transferred to the state. Now the bucking horse symbol can legally be used by any Wyoming resident to represent or promote the state.

Many residents of the Sublette County area believe that the rider on the plates is Guy Holt on Steamboat. Descendants of Holt, when introduced to old timers in that area of the state, often hear the remark, "Oh, Guy Holt, he's on the license plate."

On December 14, 1975, the National Cowboy Hall of Fame dedicated a bronze plaque commemorating Steamboat on the Hall of Fame's Roll of Great Bucking Horses. According to a Rodeo Sports News publication, the *Wild Bunch*, the B.C. Buffum classic photograph of Holt on Steamboat taken at the Albany County Fair in 1903 was used as the model for the plaque and was the model for the Wyoming license plates. A separate news item in 1978 tells of an original bronze by artist and sculptor Ridge Durand showing Steamboat and Holt that was donated to the permanent collection of the Wyoming Art Gallery, a division of the Wyoming State Museum.

"Some controversy [exists] whether Holt and Steamboat were the models for the license plates, but [it] is commonly accepted that the plate illustration was taken from a photograph of Guy Holt on Steamboat at the Albany County Fair in 1903," Durand said in that article.

However the name that is most usually touted as the model for the license emblem is that of Stub Farlow of Lander, who had no connection to Steamboat, but who was a broncho rider none-the-less. Farlow participated in the first War Bonnet Round-up held in 1913 in Idaho Falls, Idaho, where he won so many contests that he was declared "top hand" at the show.

One story about Farlow is that on a wintry night in 1944 he visited with Guy Holt. Farlow, in a somewhat inebriated state, knocked on the Holt door while Holt daughters, Gwen and Evelyn, and grandson, Ed Woodward, were there. He had come to ask Guy if he cared if he claimed that the picture on the license plate was him. Holt, being in poor health and a rather unassuming man, said he didn't care.

The 1936 license plates, the first with the bronc, were white with black letters and manufactured by the Gopher Stamp and Die Company of St. Paul, Minnesota. Then in

Wyoming vehicle license plates from 1935 to 1938. (Candy Moulton, courtesy Carbon County Motor Vehicle Department.)

1937 when the University of Wyoming celebrated its fiftieth anniversary, Hunt chose yellow and brown as the license plate colors in honor of the institution. Since then the plates have been traditionally yellow and brown, although periodically the colors have varied.

Since 1950 the Wyoming license plates have been manufactured by inmates at the Wyoming State Penitentiary "tag plant."

The argument about who the license plate rider is, and indeed if it is any specific cowboy, will no doubt go on as long as Wyomingites have breath to breathe and as long as they have heroes and loved ones to dream about.

The University of Wyoming logo varies somewhat from the one on the plates. It is generally accepted that Steamboat and Guy Holt were the models for the University of Wyoming cowboy logo in 1921 with the design taken from the Buffum photograph. Holt specifically gave his permission for the image of him to be used for that emblem.

Even though Steamboat is most often considered the symbol for Wyoming, he is not the first to be in that position.

A sorrel belonging to George N. Ostrom of Sheridan was the first horse to represent Wyoming. Ostrom was at the Sheridan rodeo in 1913 when a group of Indians was assembling horses for the one-half mile horse race. One horse was a tall, rangy sorrel mare of good breeding and very high strung.

As the race started the horses took off in a whirl of dust, but when they reached the far side of the track a young colt leaped the fence to join the sorrel mare. The race continued with the two horses neck and neck to the finish line.

Because other races were planned the Indians tried to rope the colt to return it to the corral. They had problems and Ostrom joined them, taking the colt to a stable some distance from the track. He kept the colt, naming him Red Wing.

Ostrom served with the Wyoming National Guard and during World War I found himself in charge of a baggage car at Sheridan. Ostrom, who had ridden Red Wing to the train depot, attempted to have the Army buy the horse and transport him to Cheyenne. The remount officer said Red Wing was too young. Undaunted, Ostrom built a makeshift stall in the baggage car and sneaked in Red Wing.

Ostrom's unit was stationed in Cheyenne where Red Wing, because of his style, was often used for dress parades. Ostrom once recalled the first dress parade Red Wing was in.

"In camp we had two pet bears and during the heat of the day they would stay submerged in a small lake beside the camp and as the day cooled off they would come waddling up to the kitchen for a handout. On this day, about the time of day the bears were coming to the kitchen, the regiment was all lined up to the last breath of attention on the parade ground which was directly in the path of the bears from the lake to the kitchen.

"Directly in front of the third battalion was the Major on Red Wing out to report his battalion all accounted for by a stiff salute when the two bears passed in front of Red Wing. At this point Red Wing left for the stables leaving the Major hovering in mid-air with the salute," Ostrom wrote.

From Cheyenne the unit went to North Carolina then to Bordeaux, France, where in 1918 Ostrom is said to have painted a picture on a bass drum of Red Wing bucking. At that time Red Wing was in Tours, France. The logo attracted the attention of Colonel Burke Sinclair who arranged to have a stencil made of the picture and to have plates attached to each vehicle of the 148th Field Artillery.

The logo "somehow seemed to sum up all the toughness and pride of the 148th (Field Artillery) and all their thoughts of their homes in Wyoming," one writer said. The 148th became known as the Bucking Bronco Regiment from Wyoming. Eventually the logo was used on vehicles, helmets, drinking steins, lapel buttons, and road signs. "When we got to Germany, the Germans even made jewelry with the bucking bronco on it," Ostrom wrote.

In 1973, Wyoming Governor Stanley Hathaway acknowledged Ostrom's drawing: "Now therefore be it known that the Wyoming bucking horse is dedicated to all veterans of the State and that George N. Ostrom is hereby commended for his original idea of this now famous insignia."

The license plate silhouette, the University of Wyoming logo, the bucking horse insignia of the Wyoming National Guard—all somewhat similar in design, but each with its own origin. Steamboat may be the horse on the license, he's most certainly depicted on the U. W. logo, but he is not the bronco on the National Guard insignia.

"It's got a lot of fire in that horse. The cowboy is intense, the horse is intense; they're both intense about what they're doing."

PETER M. FILLERUP IN
SOUTHWEST ART, FEBRUARY 1991

FANNING A TWISTER-STEAMBOAT

The western brand is a symbol of ownership. Seeing the scarred hide of a cow brings to mind the rank odor of singed hair, the shrill bawl of a calf, the creak of saddle leather and the grit of dirt. A brand denotes belonging.

The simple silhouette of a cowboy atop a bucking bronco is Wyoming's brand. It is on the state's license plates, lapel pins and football helmets. Cody, Wyoming, sculptor Peter M. Fillerup took that image, gave it dimension and created *FAN-NING A TWISTER—STEAMBOAT,* a heroic size sculpture placed at the University of Wyoming athletic complex to commemorate Wyoming's Centennial in 1990.

"Twister" is a hard-driving piece that shows the determination of Steamboat and his unknown rider to outlast each other. Though the cowboy is in the saddle, his perch is uncertain; the ride could go either way with success to the horse or to the man.

If the horse and rider could come to life, odds makers probably would put their money on the horse.

"We all recognize and value the symbol of Wyoming, the bucking horse, and Steamboat is legendary," Governor Mike Sullivan said. "This symbol represents the best that we have that is our heritage.... We look at that bucking horse and we all try to feel a kinship."

Steamboat came home in October of 1990 when Fillerup's sculpture was dedicated at the state's only four-year university. Steamboat is the real spirit of Wyoming, the dark-headed artist says. The horse, a natural outlaw, didn't require a bucking strap; when he went into the rodeo arena he knew his job was to throw any cowboy who had the guts to climb aboard.

Steamboat commemorates the "ruggedness, resourcefulness and independent spirit" of Wyoming people, University of Wyoming President Terry Roark said on a cold, blustery day in October when the statue was dedicated. *FANNING A TWISTER—STEAMBOAT* is "a statue not of a bucking horse, but of THE bucking horse," University of Wyoming Vice President for Development Pete Simpson said at the dedication.

"Twister" was conceived in 1983 when Fillerup did a twelve-inch bronze of a bucking horse that won acclaim at the Wyoming State Fair in 1984. The idea grew into the legendary Steamboat and a heroic statue at the University of Wyoming.

The fourteen foot tall heroic "Twister" differs from the earlier, smaller version of an unnamed bucking horse and rider. The larger version is a replica of Wyoming's legendary Steamboat complete with squared nose and flying feet. Steamboat had a unique and recognizable way of bucking by throwing his front feet one direction and his back legs another in a twisting motion, then landing with a stiff legged punch that jarred most cowboys loose and sent them flying to the ground.

This particular twisting manner, and the action of many a cowboy who took off his hat and waved it high above his head in an effort to thrill the crowd, has been captured by Fillerup. The sculpture's name comes from the action of a cowboy swinging his free arm and hat, fanning a twister.

University of Wyoming student and National Intercollegiate Rodeo Association Saddle Bronc Champion (1990) J. W. Simonson of Purdum, Nebraska, left, with Sculptor Peter M. Fillerup at the dedication of FANNING A TWISTER—STEAMBOAT. *The sculpture, placed at the University of Wyoming athletic complex during the Wyoming Centennial year, symbolizes "the ruggedness, resourcefulness and independent spirit of Wyoming people." (Candy Moulton.)*

Fillerup's sculpture depicts a "good cowboy who can fan the meanest bronc. That's the spirit of Wyoming—riding hard and fast," the artist says.

"It's got a lot of fire in that horse. The cowboy is intense, the horse is intense; they're both intense about what they're doing," Fillerup said, noting the most difficult aspect of the design was getting the gestures the way he wanted them. "It was a labor of love.... The size was part of the fun." The piece is one of the world's largest equestrian statues suspended on one foot.

"Twister" became a reality because of the vision of Fillerup and the financial and physical support of the Taggart brothers of Cody, Fillerup's hometown. Jeff, Chris and Greg Taggart underwrote the entire project. Supporting the project financially was a way for the family to give something to Wyoming, Greg Taggart said. The brothers noted that the sculpture is of a horse that has become the symbol of Wyoming and that their support was a gift to the University of Wyoming. With only one four-year university, Wyoming people come together in supporting the Cowboy athletic teams. Wyoming residents drive across the state's length and breadth to attend a university event. That feeling of support is what prompted the Taggarts to provide the money needed to bring Steamboat home to Laramie.

Besides providing financial support, the brothers came at Peter's summons when the two thousand pounds of clay arrived to be placed on the chicken-wire armature.

The brothers, some in suits and some in sensible jeans and Wyoming Cowboy t-shirts, threw clay for an afternoon, forming the basic shape of a fourteen-foot high horse and rider. The brothers left then, but Fillerup remained, moving clay this way and that until he was satisfied the nose was Steamboat's, the hat was flying properly and the cowboy's expression showed the intensity necessary to complete the ride atop the legendary bucker.

The cowboy on the fourteen-foot "Twister" wears boots and spurs, a neckerchief and angora chaps. Though dressed as cowboys of Steamboat's era would be, the man is not any particular rider, rather he is a composite of the thirty-eight men known to have climbed aboard Steamboat, including thirteen world champion broncho riders.

The piece was cast by Caleco Foundry of Cody. Proceeds from the sale of one hundred twelve-inch and twenty-one twenty-four-inch replicas of the sculpture first paid for costs associated with the heroic "Twister," and then the remainder went to the University of Wyoming Alumni Association.

The horse that thrilled rodeo crowds at the turn of the century is still giving to his native Wyoming, with the help of some dedicated friends.

PART TWO- STEAMBOAT & THE COWBOYS

"What he dœsn't know about life would fill a library, but what he knows about this great free, beautiful West would make a story to thrill your soul."

POLLY PRY, COLUMNIST, IN THE *DENVER POST*, OCTOBER 6, 1901

THOSE WONDERFUL COWBOYS

NO CLEAR RECORD EXISTS of the men who attempted to ride Steamboat; even more unclear is a record of which cowboys were successful in their rides. Certainly some cowboys stayed aboard, and at least one, Dick Stanley in 1908, rode Steamboat to a standstill. Whether he was ridden to a halt at any other time is open to speculation.

Old-time cowboys said the horse would buck his heart out then pause to catch his breath before starting again. Perhaps for some Steamboat riders, that pause was adequate to claim they had ridden the horse to a standstill. At any rate the cowboys who challenged Steamboat certainly were the best riders of the era, and their names are in the old newspaper accounts of rodeos like Cheyenne Frontier Days and the Festival of Mountain and Plain in Denver.

Many men who climbed aboard Steamboat did it while he was the "star" of the Irwin Brothers Wild West Show. Some of their efforts are recorded in various publications; no doubt others have long since been forgotten.

Steamboat was a personality to reckon with—truly the top horse of the day. Because he was so highly regarded, men who attempted to ride him, even those who bit the dust, had a feeling of pride that they'd climbed into the saddle on the back of the big black outlaw.

They told stories to their children and grandchildren of their attempt to conquer Steamboat. So by word of mouth, written word, and perhaps even a bit of folklore or legend a list of thirty-eight men who climbed on the famous horse has been ferreted out.

Those riders include thirteen world champion broncho riders, and men who went on to star in wild west shows and silent movies. Others spent their entire lives in Wyoming working on ranches. Some became ranch owners, while others went on to careers in other professions, unrelated to the cowboy way of life. Four of the cowboys have been named to the National Cowboy Hall of Fame for their contributions to the sport of rodeo.

Almost without exception the riders of Steamboat started out as everyday cowboys—men who rode vast distances on the open range gathering, sorting, and branding cows and calves. They were the real cowboys of the state that's known as the cowboy state.

About some of them little is known, and it is presumed they were riders with the Irwin Brothers Wild West Show or cowboys passing through Wyoming who drew the mighty Steamboat at one of Wyoming's fairs or rodeos. Only the best broncho busters got the chance to ride Steamboat. He was often not used in preliminary competition because top cowboys could be disqualified on him and lose the chance to become a champion.

Others who rode Steamboat are remembered by their families or were sufficiently chronicled to make it possible to tell their stories here.

ART ACORD

ART ACORD WAS A working cowboy who climbed on Steamboat's hurricane deck before he got his chance to star in silent movies in Hollywood. Acord mounted Steamboat as the result of a wager in 1910.

C.B. Irwin, along with his friend Charles Hirsig, took his broncho string to California in 1910. In Sacramento, the Happy Jack Corporation, which had previously backed broncho rider Dick Stanley, bet Irwin and Hirsig that Acord could not only ride Steamboat, but that he could whip and spur the big black horse while doing so.

Even though some had said after Stanley's ride on Steamboat at Cheyenne in 1908 and Clayton Danks' ride in Cheyenne in 1909 that Steamboat was losing his punch, one thing remained—the horse did not like to be whipped or scratched. He made that abundantly clear when Acord climbed aboard. He pitched and turned and popped Acord out of the saddle. The wager, of an unknown amount, was lost.

Even though Steamboat won that contest, Acord was a top cowboy and he won seven of eight events at the Calgary Stampede in 1916. During his rodeo career he won at least forty-two hand carved saddles, thirty-six silver mounted bridles, twenty-six pairs of chaps, plus revolvers, hats and boots by the dozen.

Records are unclear about where Acord was born, either in Utah or Stillwater, Oklahoma, but he certainly was living in Stillwater with his Mormon family by the time he was a year old in 1891. His full name was Artemus Ward Acord, and he apparently was named after humorist Artemus Ward.

Acord's early life in Oklahoma taught him about horses, cattle, guns, and fighting with his fists, all training that he called upon during his life as a cowboy, rodeo performer, and as a silent movie star in the 1920s.

Art was in New York by 1909 appearing with the Dick Stanley-Bud Atkison Wild West Show as a trick-roper, bull-dogger, and broncho buster. He had already competed in a variety of rodeos and had trophies from many of them.

While in New York, Acord landed his first job in the movie industry, as a stuntman for the Bison Film Company. He went to Big Bear Lake, California, where he supplemented his stuntwork income by writing ten dollar stories for Bison.

In 1910 he was doing stunts for the Selig Polyscope Company whose manager called him, "the greatest rider in the country, absolutely fearless and can be relied upon to tackle any stunt."

But the pay for his stunt work was modest, and in 1911 Acord joined the combined Buffalo Bill Wild West and Pawnee Bill Far East Show which was touring North America. A year later he returned to California to appear as an actor in *A Deputy's Honor—To Uphold the Law.*

In 1912 Acord was back on the screen as a telegraph operator in *The Invaders* and was an untamed heavy in *The Squaw Man* produced in 1914. In between pictures he followed the rodeo circuit winning the world bulldogging championship in Pendleton, Oregon, in 1912 with a time of twenty-four seconds. He competed at Cheyenne, Salt Lake City, and the Klamath Falls Roundup, and in 1916, he was at the Calgary Stampede where he won seven of eight events.

In 1913 Acord married actress Edythe Sterling and settled permanently in California. His home was located near that of fellow silent film star, Hoot Gibson and his wife Helen. From 1915, when he started working for Mutual Film Corporation, until 1917, when he co-starred with movie vamp Theda Bara in the Fox production of *Cleopatra,* Acord's life and career were stable. Then he and Edythe divorced, and Art went to pieces.

To take his mind off the breakup of his marriage, Acord joined the Army and served in France during World War I with the 144th and 139th infantry. He participated in the Fourth Division campaign at Verdun for which he received the Croix de Guerre and other medals. His discharge, January 24, 1919, found him still unreconciled to his divorce from Edythe Sterling and psychologically affected by the war.

Following a round of post-war victory parties with his buddies, he toured the United States and Australia with a wild west show before giving in to the lure of Hollywood once again. In 1920 he was back in motion pictures playing the lead in the Universal Pictures' fast-paced, spine-tingling western *The Moon Riders*. It was a huge success and gave Acord his first real taste of stardom.

Universal had no immediate sequel, so Acord joined his ex-wife and Pete Morrison in the production of several two-reelers for Dominant Pictures Corporation including *Call of the Blood, The Fighting Actor*, and *The Ranger's Reward.*

Acord was back with Universal in 1921 to star in *The White Horseman* which was nearly as successful and popular as *The Moon Riders*. This assured Acord a permanent niche as one of the foremost actors of the day.

However, the serial western was under siege by censors who objected to how female characters were portrayed and to the liberal use of weapons and torture in serial chapters. Production companies started changing their tone to base their stories on historical events. That led Acord to play the part of a trapper and hunter in *Winners of the West,* a story based on John C. Fremont's move west. Later productions included *In the Days of Buffalo Bill* and *The Oregon Trail,* but fans wanted the fast-paced action of earlier Acord performances. Universal reluctantly agreed to a series of action thrillers with the trick riding and fancy stunts Acord's fans demanded.

Acord had trouble coping with stardom. He couldn't control his use of alcohol and more than once was fired by Universal. He married Louise Lorraine and convinced Universal bigwigs that he was a changed man. In 1926 he made eight pictures for the company including *Sky–High Corral, Rustlers Ranch*, and *Lazy Lightning*. Five more followed in 1927.

Acord was generous with his cronies from his rodeo circuit days, often giving them cash handouts. While he was a financial and film success, his personal life was in disarray. Acord's second marriage ended in divorce. Once again Art was in the doldrums.

As a youngster back in Oklahoma, Acord learned to fight with his fists, and throughout his life he relied on them to ease tension or to get himself out of a jam.

Once in Calgary he duked it out with the Calgary Bully, a huge man feared by nearly everyone. In a bar in Calgary the bully pushed Acord aside, spilling his beer. Art didn't let the insult ride, and he challenged the giant to a fistfight. It was a rough and tumble affair that ended when Art threw an overhand right to the chin knocking the Calgary Bully out like a light.

By mid–1928 Acord fought with lightweight contender Joey Benjamin to keep in shape and to help work off depression caused by the breakup of his second marriage. It's said he used to fight all comers in the old corrals at Universal City just for the fun of it.

Although Acord tried to remain in pictures, his reputation with alcohol dogged him. At times he went on binges and couldn't be located for weeks causing havoc with production schedules. A second reason for his Hollywood demise was the fact that silent films were giving way to the new "talking" variety, and Acord's voice wasn't suitable without voice training.

A fight with a taxicab driver in October 1929 landed Acord in jail in Los Angeles. He was released on bond and headed for Mexico where he had relatives who had participated in Pancho Villa's infamous raids.

Acord performed rope tricks in Chihuahua City for a time, but soon finished his contract, spent the money on alcohol, and found himself in the company of Joe Gasper who owned a mine near Chihuahua City. Art went with Joe to the mine for a few days, then he got a job working on William Randolph Hearst's Babicorn Ranch where he remained several weeks before returning to Gasper's mine and eventually to Chihuahua City where he made several more personal appearances.

Acord was in Chihuahua City in January of 1931 when he met his death under mysterious circumstances. The official Mexican account, as recorded on his death certificate issued in Mexico, is that he died of alcohol poisoning.

But there are other versions. One is that he was killed in a barroom knifing fray. Another is that he had been whooping it up during the week between Christmas and New Year's and on January 4, 1931, died when he accidentally ingested cyanide powder. Hollywood cohorts said it was not an accident, but that Acord was murdered with cyanide.

Still another story is that he was killed when he fell from the second story window of a Chihuahua City brothel. Acord's body was returned to the United States where he was buried January 17, 1931, in Glendale, California. His gravemarker with an American Legion seal reads simply: "Our Pal, Art Acord, 1890–1931."

His western film career is marked with a star in his memory on Hollywood Boulevard. Acord's meeting with Steamboat—its macho daring, flashy wagering, and unfortunate outcome for Acord—seems a capsule summary of his life.

GEORGE ARMSTRONG

ARMSTRONG GOT HIS opportunity on Steamboat in Fort Collins, Colorado. The cowboy was a small man, only about five feet, four inches tall, and that put him at a disadvantage on Steamboat's large frame. It didn't take long for the crowd to see that Armstrong was outclassed. He was snapped off and hurt, but newspaper accounts don't reveal the type of injuries.

FRED BATH

TWO OF STEAMBOAT'S riders also played football for the University of Wyoming Cowboys. Fred Bath and Morris "Dutch" Corthell were recognized for their horseback abilities as well as their gridiron Cowboy activities. Bath got his chance to ride Steamboat on Saint Patrick's Day in 1903 at the old stockyards north of Laramie. One account of the ride says he made the ride, but only because of his strength. No other reference to Bath's effort on Steamboat has been found.

The Union Pacific had laid its rails across the country when Fred Bath arrived in Laramie in 1868. Fred was born April 8, 1868, in Boone, Iowa, and came to Wyoming with his family that same year.

Although the shiny rails of the Union Pacific were in place, Bath's father forged across Sherman Hill from Cheyenne with four oxen and a load of lumber. The lumber was used to construct Laramie's first frame building, the New

York House, one of many landmarks built by the Bath family.

"It was a frontier hotel with an old-fashioned bar in prominence, and as soon as it was erected, scores of railroad men came trooping into our hotel, singing lustily at the bar, and devouring eagerly the home-cooked meals my tired mother prepared. She cooked for a hundred men daily, and often she was without help," Bath wrote in a manuscript, "Musings of a Pioneer."

The family employed Chinese cooks, but faced constant difficulties in keeping them due to anti-Chinese labor activities. One night the hotel's stables were burned in a fire that threatened the hotel as well, and the Chinese cooks were chased from town.

At a time when Bath's mother was struggling with "endless cooking, baking, washing, and baby-tending, father was experimenting with livestock," Bath wrote. Family legend has it that the elder Bath turned his oxen onto the prairie after the family arrived in Laramie in 1868, and when spring came in 1869 the oxen were found feeding on the bottom lands of the Little Laramie River.

With the sure knowledge that the cattle could survive on the prairie, the Bath patriarch decided to claim homestead land in the valley of the Little Laramie. In 1870 he built a floorless log cabin covered with a dirt roof and complemented by a log barn and a pole corral.

A few milk cows from Iowa and some three hundred head of longhorn cattle that had been trailed from Texas gave the family a start in cattle ranching. "The cattle arrived skin and bone, and with no fences or hay we lost nearly all of them in the first wintry blizzards which thundered down upon our desolate ranch," Bath wrote.

The man who rode Steamboat and played football for the University of Wyoming had one of his first tastes of cowboy work as a lad of only eight when he and his older brother, Billy, were sent to find ninety-six horses belonging to the family. The horses were believed to have been taken by Indians. The trail led to Halleck Canyon and toward the Nebraska line. "All day we two little boys rode, always hopefully and courageously, but no Indians did we see, altho our eyes were continually searching every possible cache where they might be lurking. We eventually returned home, after an exciting chase of over a hundred miles on horseback," Bath wrote.

A few days later Billy Bath joined other ranchers in the area in another search for the horses. They trailed the horses to the Red Cloud Agency in Nebraska, but did not recover the animals because they were on the Indian reservation. It took twenty years for Bath to receive three thousand dollars as payment from the government for the ninety-six head of horses run off by the Indians.

When he was thirteen, Fred Bath ran away from home, but he was returned to his parents by a railroad worker. As punishment he was sent to live and work on the family ranch on the Laramie Plains. It was a punishment that the boy loved. During the next three years Bath looked after the stock, milked cows, churned butter for the hotel, and hauled hay and wood to town. Then when he was sixteen, his brother, Louis moved to the ranch and a foreman was hired. Having been on his own for three years, Bath disliked taking orders from a strange foreman.

Once again he took off on his own heading to North Park, Colorado, where another brother had a ranch. The two worked in North Park one winter, then Fred returned to the family ranch on the Little Laramie where he started breaking horses, a job which earned him twenty dollars a month.

In 1894 livestock prices were at rock bottom and horses were almost worthless. Fred, his father, his brother Herman, and a friend, Tom Carroll, decided to trail some of the horses to Arkansas to trade them for cattle which were worth a little more on the market. Although the need for money was great, the trip was an opportunity for the Baths and their friend to have some fun along the way.

With a herd of three hundred head of horses, they left Fort Collins, Colorado, and headed toward Denver where they went right down the main streets of town. Along the route to Pueblo, Colorado, they tried to sell the horses but found little demand for them and few offers made. The grub box was nearly empty when the decision was reached to turn the herd around and return to the Laramie Plains.

To make some money, the crew decided to put on a performance and also sold the best horse in the bunch for twenty dollars, a sum that had been turned down earlier in the trip, but that looked pretty good when there was no food. Along with being the best looking horse, the one that was sold was also the wildest.

When the purchaser said he'd like to see the horse ridden, Herman Bath did it. Then the others on the trip also did some exhibition riding and sang cowboy ballads for the audience. Their efforts netted six dollars.

With money in their pockets, the Baths turned around and headed back toward Wyoming. The trip was unexciting until after the herd passed Fort Collins.

"We were all singing and telling jokes, when suddenly the sun disappeared, and a menacing black cloud scudded across the mountain. Herman mounted his horse just as it began to sprinkle. Another larger cloud passed over the mountain. Herman put on his raincoat and started for the herd of horses. Then, thinking of me, he hastened back to the wagon, got my raincoat and started to ride towards me, singing cheerfully," Fred wrote.

But tragedy struck when Herman was almost to Fred. "A sudden blinding bolt of lightning flashed and knocked him from his horse. At that same moment fifteen of our horses went down to the ground in a heap of ringing, burning horse-flesh. Hailstones as large as eggs fell upon us, but we were too paralyzed with the shock to notice anything other than the silent form of Herman stretched beside his favorite horse—now also dead," Fred wrote.

The trip that had started with such gaiety had suddenly, irreversibly changed. Returning home was a "heartbreaking trail, the hardest road that I have ever ridden," he said.

The following year to try to ease his sorrow, Fred worked harder than ever and "to keep myself in athletic trim, I played football with the University of Wyoming's team, the Cowboys."

"My tuition was paid to the University, and although I did not have time to attend, I went to classes one day, considered myself a student, and played football each evening. The fellows drove out to the ranch for me, and after a hard day in the saddle or on the [ranch] field, I went in to practice touchdowns," Bath wrote. For three years Bath was on the Cowboy team, "During which time we were famous for our victories over Montana, Utah and Colorado."

Having played for the Cowboy football team, Bath then went on to the rodeo arena where, in 1898, he participated in the second Cheyenne Frontier Days contest, winning the World Championship in broncho riding.

But Bath's life wasn't all football, ranching and horses. He also was an accomplished musician. After his marriage, Fred taught his wife, Vallie, to play the organ so she could accompany his fiddle playing. They often drove twenty to thirty miles to a dance where they played from eight in the evening until seven in the morning, earning a dollar each.

Fred was determined to pass on his love of music to his four children, Vallie, Louis, Carl and May, and he provided them all with musical instruments and instruction. When his sister died, Fred and Vallie took in her five children, Viola, Dorothy, Orval, Gerald, and June Greaser, to raise, and these children also learned to play so the family could comprise quite a band.

Their music provided a special highlight when Fred and Vallie's oldest daughter, also named Vallie, was graduated from high school. Fred bought a school bus, loaded it with the children and their musical instruments, camping equipment and food and headed to Yellowstone National Park. While in the park they coincidentally camped near the director of the national parks who heard the band playing. He liked the music and took the Bath family to all of the lodges where they played for the guests. The children earned money from their music and received special privileges not given to ordinary tourists in Yellowstone.

Bath was determined his children should have ranches of their own, and he purchased the old ranch, with its well-known stone house, that his father had settled, for himself and Vallie. He also acquired thirty-two hundred acres of his own which could be divided among the four children. Although the family migrated to Grinnell, Iowa, so the children could receive their education, in later years Fred and Vallie returned to the old ranch. Many of the children also made their homes in Wyoming on the various Bath ranches established by their father. Bath's ride atop Steamboat was only a brief interlude in a full and active life.

HARRY BOWLES

THE LAST MAN TO CLIMB aboard Steamboat was Harry Bowles. The cowboy was working for the Irwin Brothers Wild West Show in Salt Lake City, Utah, in the fall of 1914. Bowles rode Steamboat, who did not put in his usual performance, even though he bucked harder than any other horse in the string. It would have been better for him to have thrown his rider, but the honors went to the rider on this ride, and it was destined to be Steamboat's last performance, an article in the *Laramie Republican-Boomerang* said. Not long after, Steamboat tangled with some barbed wire that led to his death.

HARRY BRENNAN

SHERIDAN, WYOMING, NATIVE Harry Brennan is often called the father of modern bronc riding because he originated the style of raking a horse from neck to cantle with his spurs. Besides his unique spurring style, Brennan also is credited with developing a set of riding rules, known as the Cheyenne Rules, from which today's customs evolved.

Harry Brennan was born in the early 1880s and was first reported aboard a bucking horse in the spring of 1901 when a troop of Negro cavalrymen at Fort McKenzie near Sheridan had trouble with a couple of rank horses which dumped the soldiers as quickly as they climbed aboard.

The commanding officer offered to pay anyone who could ride the two outlaws. Harry Brennan, the top hand for the Moncreiffe outfit, stepped forward and skillfully rode the two bucking horses, giving the people watching the show near the fort quite a performance.

Sheridan Cowboy Harry Brennan won the Denver Post Championship Belt at the 1902 competition in Denver. Shortly after the award was made, Brennan, right, and an unidentified friend rode around the arena to show off the belt. (National Cowboy Hall of Fame and Western Heritage Center.)

Brennan is known to have competed in Denver in 1901 and 1902. He captured the crown at Cheyenne in 1904 when he was named champion broncho buster of the world.

To qualify for the finals, Brennan was chosen to ride Steamboat. He had seen the black horse in action before and had made a careful study of the horse's moves. Brennan knew he needed to save himself for the last and hardest part of the campaign between horse and man. That meant he needed to ride on his spurs and not rely on the strength of his legs to grip the horse.

A newspaper account of the ride said, "Harry would hold the hackamore rope in one hand for four or five jumps and then change hands. All of the time he would keep his loose hand above his head. At this time Steamboat became winded and stopped. He stood sullenly, with his head hanging low, and when he got his wind back, his head went down between his front legs and he was off again. This second time he did not buck so long or so hard."

As Brennan finished the ride he made a move that set him apart from other riders when he took his spurs and raked them down the horse's front shoulders.

The *Wyoming Tribune* reported the championship contest this way: "Harry Brennan is a typical Wyoming cowboy. For several years he has been employed on ranches in Northern Wyoming and is one of the most popular knights of the plains in the entire state. During past wild west shows he has attracted considerable attention by the grace and ease he sits in his saddle while his mount is perfect in performing marvellous feats of gyrations and evolutions. It was Brennan who in 1902 won the first prize at the bucking contest before the Denver Horse Show."

Brennan topped Innocent Babe in his ride and "gave one of the best performances of the afternoon riding his animal to a standstill in spite of the desperate attempts of the outlaw to unseat his rider," the paper reported.

One significant event happened in conjunction with the championship contest when Bertha Keppernick of Sterling, Colorado, qualified for the championship, the first woman ever to do so. When qualifying for the championship ride, Keppernick showed her western grit and tenacity. She drew a vicious mount and within a few seconds of starting the ride was forced to pull leather and was therefore disqualified on the initial ride. However, Keppernick was given a second chance to ride the horse and had apparently subdued the animal when the horse once again went wild, tossing her over his head. Keppernick didn't stay on the ground long, instead she climbed back aboard and rode the horse until it was thoroughly exhausted and subdued, to make her qualifying round so she could compete in the finals. "Her exhibition, for a lady, was a remarkable one and the dauntless rider was cheered to the echo by the great concourse of people present."

In 1905 in Denver, Brennan rode Pinears. The *Cheyenne Daily Sun Leader* described the ride in this manner: "When the champion climbed on Pinears, Coloradoans held their breath and waited for things to happen to the daring rider. Then it must have been that veterans said, 'Oh, fudge!' Pinears reared and humped and sidled under Brennan, who laughed, it was so funny."

Besides his style, Brennan is remembered for his generosity. One story is that when he won the championship in one contest he cut the prize belt in two and gave half of it along with half of the two hundred dollar prize money to his friend Tom Minor of Idaho.

Brennan's occupation was listed as teamster in the 1907 Sheridan County Directory, and the 1908 directory reported he had moved to Butte, Montana.

In 1979 Brennan was accorded one of the top honors of any cowboy with induction into the National Cowboy Hall of Fame.

ALBERT CATON

TOLTEC, WYOMING, COWBOY Albert Caton first rode Steamboat at the Albany County Fair in 1904. Caton gave the word that he was ready, and the handlers jerked off Steamboat's blindfold. The horse took off bucking in a half-hearted way. Caton used his quirt and spurs and demonstrated a typical cowboy ride.

Steamboat did not buck very long before he stopped to gather his wind, but during that brief respite the horse found his heart. He had limbered himself up during the first heat so when Caton started to scratch and whip him as Steamboat cut loose the second time, the black horse really exploded and was out for blood.

"Caton was forced to grab the horn and called for someone to catch him, which they did before he was jarred loose from his seat," former Steamboat handler A. S. Gillespie recalled in some of his writings.

The cowboy was back in Laramie in 1905 to ride Steamboat for a prize of $54.50 that had been collected when a hat was passed. In order to get the money, however, Caton was required to whip and spur the horse on every jump until he stopped bucking; if he couldn't do so, then the money went to the horse's owners.

"Steamboat was in elegant condition when he was led out for his introduction to the crowd," Gillespie said. There he was saddled and mounted by Caton.

Steamboat seemed to squat lower than usual in order to have a gigantic first jump, and on the second leap he swapped ends which caused Caton to grab the back of his saddle. The cowboy let go of the cantle briefly, but after four wild plunges Caton was sent flying. Steamboat won the wager.

Caton was from Toltec, a community in Albany County consisting of only a post office, but little other information is known about him.

DUNCAN AND HUGH CLARK

AMONG THE EARLIEST SETTLERS in southeastern Wyoming was the Donald Clark family who emigrated to the area from Canada in the spring of 1874. Sons Duncan and Hugh both had connections to Steamboat.

Donald Clark and his wife Jane McPhee both were born in Scotland, but they were married in Egremont, Canada, in 1865 where they farmed until hearing from Jane's brother, Donald McPhee, of the opportunity in the Wyoming territory.

Upon arrival in Wyoming, Donald Clark claimed a 160-acre homestead on Upper Horse Creek between Cheyenne, Chugwater, and Laramie. He immediately started building a home for his family, but before it was completed winter arrived, and Clark headed for Canada where he got Jane and their five children, Neil, Flora, Angus, Catherine, and Duncan.

Later, at the Wyoming homestead, five more children were born: Mary Ann, Margaret, Donald, Sarah, and Hugh.

Duncan Clark, the fifth child, was a well-known ranch hand and cowboy, and his youngest brother, Hugh, may have tried to emulate his older brother as he also took to ranch work and competing in rodeos. Though no record exists that indicates Duncan ever climbed aboard Steamboat, he is credited with obtaining the horse from the Two Bar for John Coble's bucking string.

After the family was established in Wyoming, tragedy struck when a typhoid epidemic in 1887 claimed the lives of

Mary Ann, then age twelve, and Angus, age sixteen. Nine members of the family had typhoid, and it took most of the winter for them to recover.

Donald Clark was a visionary who wanted to see as many cattle on the range with his DC brand as possible. He eventually expanded his ranch from the 160-acre homestead to an operation of more than eight thousand acres.

With a ranch that large, Clark thought it important that his family have a fine house, so he built a fifteen-room home of gray native stone. Following its completion, the house was often the site of parties and dances for neighbors in the area.

It was on that large ranch that Hugh Clark learned about cattle and horses. He also worked for the Swan Land and Cattle Company's Two Bar Ranch.

Hugh was at Cheyenne Frontier Days in 1903 where he was the first man to ride. He'd been pegged by the *Denver Post* as the favorite in the broncho busting contest, even though he was only nineteen years old. His mount was Teddy Roosevelt. The horse bucked very high and hard for a short distance, then the loose belt of Clark's chaps got caught in the saddle horn, forcing him to seize the horn to release himself. He was disqualified.

That same year Clark, Buffalo Vernon, and Pecos Craver gave the best exhibitions of trick roping ever seen in Cheyenne, local newspapers reported. They caught running horses and mounted men in all manner of positions, even roping a running horse by the tail.

Clark got his first known shot at Steamboat in 1904. Steamboat handlers, including A. S. Gillespie, were taking the horse from Cheyenne to Laramie for the Albany County Fair when they stopped for the night at the Donald Clark Ranch. Several people at the ranch wanted to see Hugh ride Steamboat, but the horse's handlers refused. A deal was cut,

Pecos Craver, Hugh Clark, and Buffalo Vernon sometimes teamed up to give exhibitions of trick roping. Here Pecos Craver keeps a rope spinning above his head as he reclines on the arena ground. (American Heritage Center, University of Wyoming.)

however, and plans were made for Clark to ride Steamboat when the horse was on his way back from Laramie.

The return trip didn't include a stop at the Donald Clark Ranch. Instead the overnight rest was at the MacDonald Ranch on Pole Creek. Hugh Clark went there to claim his ride.

An account of the ride by Gillespie says, "We saddled Steamboat out in an alfalfa stubble field. Before Hugh mounted, he asked if Bill Frazee and I would catch Steamboat in case he [Hugh] hollared [sic] for us. We held Steamboat until Hugh Clark was seated and told us to 'let him go.' As we let him go we sprang for our pickup horses, for Steamboat was 'leaving those parts,' and Hugh had hollered for us to pick him up. Steamboat was moving so fast and jumping so crooked and swapping ends so often that Bill Frazee and I could not get a hold of him. Finally, Steamboat swapped ends right into the side of Bill Frazee's horse and Bill grabbed the hackamore rope. Then I spurred my horse up to the other side and took another hold on Steamboat. Hugh Clark had lost both stirrups and was over on one side of the horse with his leg dragging in the alfalfa."

The Fourth of July in 1905 found Clark in Rawlins where he got his second try at Steamboat. He lasted about six jumps before pickup men Gillespie and Ben Roberts were hailed. "We closed in on Steamboat from each side and each of us dallied the hackamore rope around our saddle horns and soon pulled Steamboat's head up," Gillespie said. The ride was good for first place for Clark.

In 1905 Clark was competing in Cheyenne again where he tied for the world champion broncho buster title along with Sam Scoville. Clark got a twenty-five dollar cash award, a pair of boots worth the same amount, a ten dollar pair of spurs, and the second place prize awards. Scoville got the $450 saddle donated by the Union Pacific Railroad.

MORRIS CORTHELL

MORRIS "DUTCH" CORTHELL was a mainstay of the University of Wyoming varsity football backfield in 1909 and as a hobby rode bucking horses, including Steamboat at the Albany County Fair in 1910. Like Fred Bath, he found both football and broncs to his liking.

"I remember that I got two surprises that day in 1910: the first was when my name was drawn to ride Steamboat; the second and even greater surprise was that I was still in the saddle at the end of the ride. Just before I started to mount I was having an argument with some friends as to whether I'd stay two or three jumps," Corthell recalled in a letter in 1952.

For Corthell's ride on Steamboat in 1910, the men holding Steamboat let the horse loose just as Dutch started to mount. Corthell got into the saddle, but couldn't catch his right stirrup. Steamboat didn't stand around waiting for Corthell to get set. Instead, the horse took off toward the judges' stand. Then he bucked down to the race track where he turned and made a circle past the horse corrals.

People in the crowd jumped to their feet because of the intense excitement and also because, as a local boy, Corthell was well-known.

Corthell had to grab the horn when Steamboat made a vicious turn to the left just before the outrider picked up the cowboy. When the contest was over the judges had difficulty in determining the winner, so they put the names of the top four riders into a hat and selected the winner with a draw from the hat. Corthell's name wasn't drawn, so he was out of the prize money.

Even so, many felt his ride was the best and that he should have received first place for his effort atop Steamboat.

"Before I rode him, there was always a question when I tackled a bronc of whether I could ride him. After my ride on Steamboat I felt perfectly confident when I tackled any other bronc," Corthell wrote.

"I think the outstanding recollections that I have are that Steamboat was a native; as a young horse he roamed the western country, largely the part of the West which furnished most of the talent, both horses and riders, for Cheyenne Frontier Days. As a bucking horse, he was a natural. So far as I ever saw him in action or heard of his performances, he never quit bucking as long as there was a saddle on his back, except to stop to get his wind. Then too, he was a true bucker. He didn't have to have a flank cinch to get him to do his stuff. He had about everything a bucking horse could have, speed, crooked jumps, and when he hit the ground, the rider got jolted plenty," Corthell wrote.

At the time Dutch got his chance on Steamboat, the Laramie man was attending the University of Wyoming. In 1909, he had made his mark as a star on the University of Wyoming football team. Corthell eventually completed his education and was a prominent attorney in Laramie. His long career was greatly involved with the protection and development of water rights for ranches in the Laramie valley and the adjudication of interstate water rights.

WILLIAM "PECOS" CRAVER

CHEYENNE FRONTIER DAYS 1899 found William "Pecos" Craver out riding all other broncho busters. Although prior to 1902 there was no world championship, generally the cowboy who topped the pack in Cheyenne was considered the title holder.

Craver made a name for himself as a trick roper and western rider. He performed with the Buffalo Bill Wild West Show and drew attention with his ride on Steamboat in 1904 when he climbed aboard the mighty bucker in Laramie wearing a pair of beaded moccasins, rather than solid cowboy boots.

Though he was a top hand, Craver quickly found Steamboat was not the kind of horse to take lightly, and riding in moccasins was not a good idea.

Pecos competed in Frontier Days in Cheyenne in 1904 then headed over the mountain to Laramie for the Albany County Fair where he immediately requested the chance to ride Steamboat. Pecos had previously worked for John Coble and went directly to him to ask that he be allowed to ride the

William "Pecos" Craver shows fine style aboard Steamboat in this ride at the 1904 Albany County Fair. However, the powerful horse threw Craver to the ground after a series of jolting jumps. (American Heritage Center, University of Wyoming.)

horse. Whether it was because of Coble or not, Pecos got his shot on the big black horse.

Before his ride Craver was doing his fancy rope tricks and when it was time to saddle Steamboat he did so, still wearing the beaded moccasins he had worn for his roping exhibition. Craver must have underestimated Steamboat's power and ability as a bucker, or he surely would have taken time to switch from moccasins to boots and spurs.

When Craver had saddled and mounted, Steamboat was let loose and "Pecos went into action with his quirt and surely hit Steamboat hard, as the 'wallops' could be heard all over the fairgrounds."

Steamboat twisted and turned for nearly a dozen jumps then he turned end-for-end and bounced off to one side, nearly splitting Pecos in two. The rider was still aboard, however, and Steamboat jumped to the right and left, sunfishing and finally turning end-for-end again. That was enough to send Craver flying to the ground where he lit on his feet, completely out of breath. Steamboat didn't stop then, but continued to try to get the saddle off until he was stopped by pick-up men.

Craver's wife was also a trick roper, and the two often performed together. They were at Frontier Days in 1906 when the *Wyoming Tribune* reported the "champion fancy ropers of the world, and who have appeared on two continents with Buffalo Bill's Wild West Shows, were on hand to give an exhibition of rope throwing which was a revelation to the effete Easterners."

CLAYTON DANKS

ONE OF THE HIGHLIGHTS OF Clayton Danks' career was at the 1909 Cheyenne Frontier Days when he rode Steamboat to his second World Championship. The man and the horse had met before and they rose to fame together.

Danks was born in O'Neill, Nebraska, July 21, 1879, the son of John and Sarrah Gregg Danks. His parents were of English, Irish, Scotch, and Dutch descent. Danks was from a large family including sisters Anna and Lula and brothers Harry, Peter, James, Lawrence and his twin, John. At five feet, nine inches tall and weighing just 130 pounds, Danks was slim, wiry, and quick as a cat. His balance was like that of a tightrope walker.

When Clay, as he was called, was about five, the family moved to a ranch they had purchased near Chadron, Nebraska. It was there that Clay and his brothers rode their first bronchos. Danks spent his first years herding cattle and breaking horses, sometimes riding more than a hundred horses a week.

In 1896 Danks came to Wyoming, but it wasn't until about 1903 that he began to take rodeo seriously. He was working at the Bosler Ranch at the time where he first saw Steamboat, the horse that would rise to fame with him in rodeo.

Danks rode the black horse that year at the Cheyenne Frontier Day, but first place went to Guy Holt who was on Young Steamboat. In September of 1903 the two Wyoming cowboys had a head-to-head competition promoted by C. B. Irwin and E. J. Bell who went through the grandstands at the Albany County Fair in Laramie collecting money for the prize. They gathered seventy dollars which they agreed to split between Holt and Danks with thirty dollars to go to each cowboy and ten dollars to the worst horse of the exhibition.

For the contest, Danks rode first and he mounted Steamboat. "Clayton Danks got firmly in the saddle before Steamboat was released from his blindfold. As usual the outlaw took a good look around before commencing proceedings, then up went his back into an arch like an angry cat, his tail went between his hind legs and his head between his front legs and he was ready to begin. He bucked in a circle for a few minutes then ahead and with the same wicked twist and wrench of the back that is characteristic of the worst horses.

"Danks sat up straight, swung with the motion of the horse and rode splendidly. Only once when Steamboat gave an extra sharp twisting buck at the rails, did he appear in any danger of coming off, but he righted himself quickly. Danks

Clayton Danks sits tight atop Steamboat in a competition and fans the big horse with his hat. Danks won the World Championship Broncho Riding title in 1909 by riding Steamboat. (American Heritage Center, University of Wyoming.)

rode with his hands down and a strong grip on the hackamore rope, this made some people think that he was 'pulling leather' but he never touched the saddle with his hands," a newspaper account of the ride said.

In an article for *Frontier Times* in 1962, the cowboy said, "That horse was interwoven in my life. The first one to handle Steamboat was my brother, so that bronc had a special interest to my family. Jimmy didn't handle Steamboat long...before he knew he had a natural outlaw on his hands."

"In my opinion, Steamboat was the hardest bucker of all times. He never needed a flank cinch, and was always ready for his man. He had a powerful punch.

"Steamboat was dynamite. Steamboat was a self-propelled trajectory. He was a kite that turned inside out and showed the rider the bottoms of four hooves. He was flying mane under you, and a projectile that put you halfway across the arena in four jumps. He was a volcanic eruption of sound as well as fury while he was doing it."

The horse was hard to ride because of the way he hit the ground. "There are other bucking horses that do more fancy pitching, but Steamboat just keeps his head down and fights. When he gives one of those peculiar twisting jumps and comes down stiff-legged, the man is rocked something painful. I had my head snapped back until I thought it was going to come off, and I felt as if my lungs were going to burst when I had ridden that horse for a few jumps," Danks told *Frontier Times*.

In 1903 Danks had his second or third introduction to Steamboat. He rode the horse on the Laramie-area Dunn Ranch, and by the second ride the horse was "in there pitching to throw me," Danks said. "That determination of his is what padded my pocket with gold, and I do mean gold. In those days, that's just what we received in payment. At the big Elks' Convention in 1906 held in Denver, Steamboat put $500 in gold in my pockets."

"Don't let me give the impression I was the only bronc peeler to stay aboard Steamboat. Although he was one of the broncs ridden the fewest times to a qualified finish, there were riders who tested his mettle and stuck with him," Danks noted in *Frontier Times*.

Besides his skill on bronchos, Danks was handy with a rope and, in 1904, was declared the World Champion Steer Roper. In fact, if there had been an all-around title given, Clayton Danks certainly could have won it, because, after seeing Will Pickett bulldog a steer, he began to perfect that art, too.

Pickett, a black man from Taylor, Texas, was the talk of rodeo in 1904. He worked at the 101 Ranch, later performed with the Irwin Brothers Wild West Show, and according to a news story at the time, did "without a device or appliance of any kind, attack a fiery wild-eyed and powerful steer, dashing under the breast of the great brute, turn and sink his strong ivory teeth into the underlip of the animal." Pickett would throw his shoulder against the neck of the brute, causing it, under the strain of a slowly bending neck, to quiver, tremble, and then sink to the ground.

Danks practiced and then helped perfect the method that is used in steer wrestling today. Early on, the cowboy bit the lip or nose of the steer to force it to the ground, but later he shifted to the modern method of twisting the steer's neck to force the animal over. Once Danks said he tried to be as good or better than Pickett. "And I tried to be decent about it. I always brushed my teeth before I went bulldogging."

The talented cowboy won two saddle bronc riding world championships, in 1907 and 1909, the first time riding Millbrook and the second time on Steamboat.

Danks married Marie Fitger, April 27, 1905, in Casper, Wyoming. She had been born in Salt Lake City, Utah, November 23, 1883, and moved to Wyoming in 1886 with her parents Danial R. and Cynthia Nielson Fitger. She attended school in Casper and had a brother, Eugene, and two sisters, Lillian and Christine.

Marie was a well-known cowgirl often competing in the ladies' relay races at Cheyenne Frontier Days and other rodeos. She was a world champion relay race rider. Both Clayton and Marie were regular performers with the Irwin Brothers Wild West Show. Danks once signed to ride with the Buffalo Bill Wild West Show, but he never got the chance to perform because there was such a great response from cowboys wanting to ride for Buffalo Bill that Danks, like other younger cowboys, was left out in favor of older, more seasoned riders.

After Danks retired from the rodeo arena and as a wild west show star, he worked on numerous ranches in Wyoming, including the Dumbell, the Iron Mountain Ranch Company, the H. A. Chapman spread on the Sweetwater, and the Reverse Four Cattle Company.

Danks then turned to a career in law enforcement. He was the police chief in Parco, Wyoming, now Sinclair, for seven years. In 1936, he moved to Lander, Wyoming, where he was sheriff of Fremont County for sixteen years. In his later years he enjoyed reminiscing about his days in the rodeo arena.

"When Steamboat's day was over, I think a part of rodeo ended for me, too. I missed that black beneath me the way you miss a partner who has grubstaked you for years," Danks said. Danks died in June of 1970.

JAMES T. DANKS

THE TOP HAND ON THE Swan's Two Bar Ranch, James T. (Jimmy) Danks was the first man to ever climb aboard Steamboat. Their contest took place on the range with no cheering crowds to honor the performance. Jimmy is said to have ridden Steamboat five times.

Danks was a brother of Clayton Danks who went on to win two world championship broncho riding titles, including one on the back of Steamboat. Jimmy Danks rode Steamboat on several occasions but could never "get him off center."

"I guess he thought bucking was his business," the range rider once said. More information about the horse and Danks' bouts with Steamboat is included in Chapter Two of this book.

Although he competed at Cheyenne Frontier Days, Jimmy Danks' life is not so clearly chronicled as that of his brother Clayton. He was a cowboy all his life, working for the Swan Land and Cattle Company for many years. He was one of the very top men that ranch had from its beginning. Danks learned how to sort and classify the prime fat beef which was shipped after each round-up, and he was often summoned by the general manager of the Swan outfit to assist in selecting the beef.

One old timer said of Jimmy Danks, "He will tell you himself that he could outride Clayton. However, he did not take rodeoing up for a livelihood as Clayton did. His cowboying was out on the range and his work and he was at all times working for the interest of his employers. He was not making his horses buck to get practice nor did he practice roping steers and tying them down for practice. He got his practice at his every day work."

Jimmy did ride bronchos at rodeos however, including Cheyenne Frontier Days in 1903 where he placed fourth on Little Tex. His horse bucked straight forward toward the corral, and did not make much of an exhibition until he was turned back toward the field, when he did some very wicked pitching, sunfishing several times.

Jimmy married Rose Mellima and in later years made his home in Ardmore, South Dakota, and then in Fort Collins, Colorado.

JOHNNIE DODGE

ALTHOUGH STEAMBOAT PERFORMED at Cheyenne Frontier Days, often he wasn't ridden until the finals because the horse was so powerful he could unseat a top rider, therefore spoiling any chance for a world championship.

As previously recounted in Chapter Seven, in 1907 the preliminary competition was stiff, but finally the judges decided the contest lay between Johnnie Dodge and Clayton Danks. The men drew horses with Danks drawing Millbrook and Dodge Steamboat.

Dodge climbed aboard and stayed with the big horse until the cowboy was almost exhausted. Then Steamboat began a new series of contortions which finally dumped the weakened rider over the horse's head. After that it was simply a question of Danks sticking to Millbrook to win his first world championship.

The old time cowboys all agreed Steamboat was at his prime in 1906 and 1907, so if the luck of the draw had given Danks Steamboat instead of Dodge, the championship also might have switched hands.

While Danks went on to win another championship title in 1909, newspapers make no further mention of Dodge.

FRED "CYCLONE" DODGE

FRED "CYCLONE" DODGE IS a man with a mysterious past. Although Dodge always claimed to have been born in Cheyenne November 20, 1888, his family isn't sure if that is a fact.

Wherever and whenever Fred Dodge was born, one thing remains certain, at a young age he developed the ability to ride the twisting, bucking back of a broncho.

Dodge carried with him a collection of newspaper clippings related to broncho riding, including snippets about himself and other cowboys riding in various rodeos. One mentioned he was forced to "grab leather' atop Steamboat, although little more is known of that ride.

In the Ak-Sar-Ben Omaha special bucking contest at Cheyenne Frontier Days in 1910, Dodge placed second behind John Rick. Dodge rode Cotton Eye Joe.

Other references to Dodge's ability as a bucking horse rider are evident in clippings, though dates and places aren't always known.

For example one said, "As brilliant as McCarty's performance was against a tough antagonist, was Fred Dodge's ride on Billy the Kid, an outlaw as vicious as was he whose name has been conferred upon him. The Kid is a terrific sunfisher with an ambition to bump the stars, but Dodge was still there whenever the horse and the earth reconnected and he was still there when the Kid grew sulky and quit in disgust."

Yet another clipping noted that "Lost Chance fought terrifically to unseat Dodge but the rider stuck tight."

Besides being a top hand, Dodge was a determined man often climbing aboard a pitching horse even though he was injured. One report said, "The most courage was shown by Fred Dodge who had already sustained a dislocated knee when he insisted on riding the horse he had drawn, 'Wild Cat.' The horse proved to be a vicious and difficult bucker, but Dodge stayed with him until he fell and the rider's knee was again injured."

Still another account of that ride said, "Fred Dodge, who had a leg badly hurt in the burro riding contest, and who was brought to the city for treatment, returned and later rode 'Wild Cat' in the bucking contest."

Dodge was in New York in 1912 where he worked as a fireman for the New York, New Haven and Hartford Railroad Company. In 1912 and 1913 Dodge rode with the Buffalo Bill and Pawnee Bill Wild West Shows. His reputation was extremely good. An October 28, 1912, letter of recommendation from G.W. Lillie, better known as Pawnee Bill, said, "We have found him to be a thoroughly experienced horseman, sober, reliable and an excellent cowboy."

The next spring, they recommended Dodge as a "first-class rider." And another recommendation from Duke R. Lee said, "Mr. Dodge is one of the few genuine cowhands in the business, good clean slick rider and straight roper, sober, hard worker and good dresser."

When he was hired to ride for Buffalo Bill and Pawnee Bill, Dodge was required to ride in all acts and furnish his own outfit including a pair of Colt Forty-fives.

Dodge joined the Navy in Denver during World War I and served on the destroyer McCormick from November 23, 1917, until September 19, 1919. Following his release from the service he immediately re-enlisted, this time in the Naval Air Service. He served in that division of the Navy until October 10, 1921, and was stationed at Coco Solo, Panama Canal Zone. There he did some deep sea diving and tested Navy aircraft.

While in Panama, Dodge was involved in a crash landing of an airplane. He wrote to William C. Dodge of New York that the plane he was in had fallen one thousand feet in the Canal Zone but that he was uninjured. Dodge said he and his companions had "some landing, with the machine in flame."

It is William C. Dodge who gives Fred Dodge the aura of mystery. The wealthy businessman referred to Fred as his son, yet Dodge always claimed to have been born in Wyoming and when William C. Dodge died, no mention was made of Fred Dodge as a surviving son. Fred's relatives say they simply don't know what the connection was, nor the true story of his heritage and birth. They believe his parents were Fred and

Elisabeth Dodge and that his birth was in Cheyenne. His family further thinks he was reared in Westfield, New Jersey.

Upon receiving his discharge from the Navy, Fred returned to Colorado where on February 6, 1922, he married Eileen Puckett. He was thirty-three years old and she was nineteen. They soon moved to Saratoga, Wyoming, to make their home. They had three daughters, Eileen, Dorothy, and Doris. Dorothy died as a child, a victim of scarlet fever and pneumonia.

Dodge worked a variety of jobs while living in Saratoga. He worked on ranches, in the timber industry, and also did a variety of odd jobs. He helped build the highway from Walcott Junction, Wyoming, to Saratoga. His interest in rodeo continued, and Fred assisted with the Fourth of July celebration in Saratoga. At the time of his death, March 31, 1937, he was working in construction.

Dodge had been in a despondent condition prior to his death and was found by his wife and daughter in the coal shed near their home. He had shot himself twice through the stomach using a small thirty-two caliber pistol. Although Dodge was taken to the Memorial Hospital in Rawlins, his injuries were fatal. Burial was in Saratoga.

PAUL HANSEN

PAUL HANSEN IS BELIEVED to be the rider who climbed aboard Steamboat more than any other bronc peeler. He rode for several seasons with the Irwin Brothers Wild West Show, and in a 1952 letter said he climbed aboard Steamboat as many as fifty or sixty times. "One time, I started to whip him when I was riding him at Grand Forks, North Dakota. Steamboat would not be whipped and he threw me." Hansen was one of the men present when Steamboat was killed in 1914. He was later a deputy sheriff in Laramie County.

PAUL (MIKE) HASTINGS

OFTEN CALLED THE GREATEST bulldogger of rank cattle in the world, Paul (Mike) Hastings cut his teeth on bucking horses, performed with the Irwin Brothers Wild West Show, was the 1931 Steer Wrestling Champion at Cheyenne Frontier Days, and was the 1974 honoree of the Rodeo Historical Society in the National Cowboy Hall of Fame.

He rode Steamboat as a member of the Irwin Brothers company, but no specific details about any of his rides on the black horse are available.

Born the son of a saloon keeper in Casper, October 23, 1891, Hastings ran away from home when he was eleven and started riding range bucking horses when he was fifteen. He started working with C.B. Irwin when he was only seventeen, and as an eighteen-year-old he participated in both broncho riding and bulldogging at Cheyenne Frontier Days.

Well-known as a top bulldogger, Hastings is also remembered for his horses Stranger and Sport who helped many cowboys take home pay checks. Sport often was used to haze a steer for a cowboy riding Stranger, the horse Hastings bought for six hundred dollars from another bulldogger. Once when Hastings was offered thirty-six hundred dollars for the horse, he refused to sell.

By 1916 it was clear that Hastings' specialty was steer wrestling. He rode Stranger up to the running steer then used a "Tarzan" lock on the horns as Stranger continued to run,

Early-day bulldoggers used their teeth to bite the upper lip of a steer and pull it over, as demonstrated here by Mike Hastings who was called the Iron Man of bulldogging. (National Cowboy Hall of Fame and Western Heritage Center.)

dropping the burly dogger with his feet well forward. His skill and power helped him set a record at Guy Weadick's Stampede in New York City when he successfully landed a steer in eleven seconds.

Hastings also was a top judge of bucking stock and discovered the great horse Hells Angels harnessed and mowing hay with another horse in Montana. Hells Angels is one of five bucking horses honored by the National Cowboy Hall of Fame. Hastings worked as a chute boss, stock foreman, and bucking horse scout or buyer for Colonel W. T. Johnson for many years and also was employed for a time by Gene Autry Rodeos handling similar duties.

For twenty-five years, from 1940 until he died in 1965, Hastings worked as foreman at the Cimarron Ranch near Putnam Valley, New York.

When he was inducted into the Rodeo Hall of Fame it was said that "Mike Hastings was a behind-the-scenes maker of champions. His sixth sense of impending danger in the rodeo arena saved the lives of many young cowboys and rodeo stock alike. Although rough as an uncut diamond, Mike was beloved by all who have a deep feeling for rodeo."

GUY HOLT

GUY HOLT'S TALENT WITH horses began when he was young and continued throughout his life. Early in his career, he made a name for himself by riding Steamboat at the Albany County Fair in Laramie. A pencil-written letter written by his wife, Annie Jo, in 1946 to the *Wyoming State Tribune*, says Holt rode Steamboat seven times.

His father, Thomas D. Holt, had been orphaned as a boy in Texas and had been in the Cheyenne area as early as 1876, driving freight wagons for a time between Deadwood, South Dakota, and Sydney, Nebraska, before returning to Texas.

In 1880 Thomas returned to Wyoming, working as a wrangler for one of the cattle herds coming up the Chisholm Trail. In 1882 he married Mary Lannon whose family was early pioneers from Illinois.

Their son Guy Edward was born December 5, 1883, at his grandfather Lannon's ranch near Cheyenne. Not much is known about his boyhood. Guy attended school at Hecla,

In 1903 Hecla, Wyoming, cowboy Guy Holt was named World Champion Broncho Rider at Cheyenne Frontier Days. He won this saddle as part of his prize. Holt later was selected as the Most Popular Cowboy of Wyoming in a contest sponsored by the Cheyenne newspaper. He ranched most of his life at Hecla, Cora, and Jackson, Wyoming. (Flossie Moulton Collection.)

west of Cheyenne. Hecla was a copper mining area in the 1880s, and at the time, it was home to a copper smelter and a brick kiln.

Guy's father was the foreman for the McGee-Haygood outfit, but in 1890, he acquired a ranch in the same area of South Crow Creek. Three boys and three girls in the Holt family grew to adulthood, and Guy was the oldest. The family's transportation and recreation centered around horses, so the boys turned to riding, racing, and roping contests. They gathered at different ranches to display their prowess. It was the natural thing then, to compete at Cheyenne's Frontier Days, which had begun in 1897.

The date Guy first entered the broncho riding contest at Frontier Days is not known, but 1903 was his year for the headlines. He won the World Championship Broncho Rider contest during the last week of August, riding Young Steamboat—the horse that was a half-brother to the famed Steamboat. Holt also rode many times in Laramie at the Albany County Fair and in Douglas at the Wyoming State Fair.

Along with the world title in 1903, Holt also won the Festival of Mountain and Plain belt that had been won in 1901 and 1902 by Thad Sowder. Holt didn't get to keep the belt since it had to be won by the same cowboy three times before it became his possession. The organizers of the Mountain and Plain Festival didn't sponsor the event after 1903, and the belt eventually wound up in the Kuykendall collection displayed at the Colorado State Museum

Holt, like many cowboys of the era, worked for Charlie Irwin on the Y6 Ranch for a time, and one story goes that Irwin had a standing bet of one thousand dollars in gold to anyone who could outride Guy Holt.

Holt made much of his reputation with his ride on Old Steamboat at the Albany County Fair in September of 1903.

Although Guy didn't win the contest, he took second behind Ed Danks, a brother of Clayton and Jimmy Danks. The event was recorded permanently by University of Wyoming Professor B.C. Buffum in a photograph and became the model for the University of Wyoming logo and perhaps the bucking horse on the Wyoming license plates [*see Chapter Nine*].

Holt's ride was described by one early-day writer this way: "When Steamboat had been saddled in the usual manner, Guy Holt mounted him with all his confidence based on past honors. When Guy was seated in the borrowed saddle, which he was not used to, he gave the word to let him go—did Steamboat go—He bucked the hardest that anyone had ever seen him buck with a rider aboard. Steamboat showed more viciousness in his bucking than he ever had done in his entire colorful career."

A newspaper account of the ride said, "Steamboat looked fat and saucy, in very different shape than when he was ridden here last March, he stood as usual quietly when being saddled, but immediately [after] his blind was removed he began to pitch in wicked fashion. His trick jumping is very hard to sit, though he does not rise far from the ground, in as much as he twists everytime when in the air, and gives a jerk that few horses ever learn.

"Guy Holt lost his right stirrup the second jump, and at the third jump grabbed the horn and pulled leather for all that he was worth. Once only did he leave hold of that horn and make a half-hearted attempt to whip his mount, but he soon grabbed the horn again and finally lost both reins and clung with both hands. It is but fair to state that Holt rode in a strange saddle, with only one cinch, where as he is accustomed to two cinches."

It has been recorded by some cowboys of the day that Guy was badly hurt during the ride. As one said, "He was damn near killed." The injury came, apparently because of the borrowed saddle but its severity is not recorded in any records. The same day, Holt won the green horse race, but he took two bad falls in that contest as well. The first fall happened in front of the grandstand just after Holt mounted when he was pitched over the head of his horse, and the second tumble came after he had won the race and while he was taking his animal to the stable. The horse made a dash for the fence and laid Holt over in the paddock.

Even so, the following day Holt and Clayton Danks competed in a head-to-head competition promoted by C.B. Irwin and E.J. Bell. Danks rode Steamboat "with his hands down and a strong grip on the hackamore rope, this made some people think that he was 'pulling leather' but he never touched the saddle with his hands," a newspaper report said.

Holt then stepped up to ride Teddy Roosevelt. An account of the ride said, "Holt rode his own saddle this time and was careful to get a good seat before the horse was turned loose. 'Teddy' bucks much higher off the ground and 'sunfishes' in the area, but does not have quite the same trick of twisting as Steamboat.

"Holt gave a very different exhibition to his performance the day before. He rode prettily and well, whipped his mount repeatedly; did not pull leather or show any signs of coming off, and gave as good an exhibition as did Danks. He was loudly cheered when he dismounted. His ride was the more meritorious as he was suffering from several bad hurts from his experience of the previous day." However, Holt placed second, behind Danks that day, and later when he rode Steamboat again in 1904 at Cheyenne, the championship went to Harry Brennan.

The injuries Holt received in Laramie certainly weren't the only ones that came as a result of his broncho riding career. Once he was helping saddle a horse when the hack-amore caught up high on the chute and had to be cut. "Guy standing tip-toe used such force in cutting the rope on the hackamore he cut his arm also. Guy paid little attention to his arm 'til after the show. And without any supper he went to a doctor, who took three or four stitches with what Guy thought was a very dull needle, so he fainted. But I thought he shouldn't have expected Guy to stand while he sewed him up," Guy's wife, Annie, wrote in a 1952 letter.

Holt married Annie Jo Gearheart on December 10, 1904. According to a newsclipping announcing their marriage, they were a popular young couple of the area who, knowing the playfulness of their friends, chose to be married at the Gear-heart home at Sherman, Wyoming. The town no longer exists, but was where the Ames monument is today.

Annie Jo had been born at Tie Siding, Wyoming, south of Laramie and was an early student in the building now known as Old Main at the University of Wyoming. She first met Guy Holt while visiting her sister Addie, who was teaching at the Granite Canyon School. Their courtship evolved somewhat around the rodeo life. Annie Jo was a small lady and always had poor eyesight. She and sister Addie were very close and usually attended rodeos together.

Those were the days before public address systems were used for announcing riders. The men of the day usually wore white shirts with occasionally a colored neckerchief, but were still sometimes hard to distinguish. To help Jo see which was her "fella," Addie, who was an expert seamstress, made Guy a robin's egg blue shirt. It caused considerable talk, such that it was written about by Polly Pry, a columnist for the *Denver Post*. Each rodeo after that, cowboys appeared in more colored shirts. That was the beginning of the colorful western shirts. Guy's favorite was a red turtleneck.

In 1905 the *Wyoming State Tribune* had a contest to find the most popular cowboy. Two separate votes were taken. Fans from Laramie County were counted in one poll and the other ballot included votes from all of Wyoming. Guy Holt was the winner in both polls. His prize was an all expense paid trip to the Lewis and Clark Exposition in Portland, Oregon. Another year, he won second in the popularity contest and, with the title, a pair of spurs.

After their marriage, Guy and Annie Jo lived at the Holt Ranch on South Crow Creek. Among other things, Guy and his brothers, David (Pat) and Eugene broke and sold horses for the soldiers at Fort D. A. Russell. While Guy was making his reputation on the hurricane deck of bucking bronchos, Pat was close by working as a pick-up man at the Cheyenne Frontier Days celebration for seventeen years.

Guy and Jo had seven children, five of whom grew to adulthood: Gwen, Evelyn, Tom, Florence, and Ethel. Being a father and having family responsibilities brought Guy to the realization that the business of riding bucking horses was too risky, so he didn't participate in rodeos as much after his marriage. However, in 1908 Guy and Jo took their two little girls, Gwen and Evelyn, by train to North Platte, Nebraska, to watch Guy participate in Buffalo Bill's Wild West Show.

Holt spent his entire life in ranching and always had horses around. The city of Cheyenne appropriated the waters of Crow Creek in 1905, and the value of the Holt ranch was seriously affected. They filed suit against the city, but lost. The suit remains a precedent in Wyoming water law today. Because of the loss of the water the entire Holt family moved to the Pinedale, Wyoming, country in 1911 and established a ranch near Cora. A partnership was formed with the father and sons, but it ended in financial disaster because of a very dry year and very high hay prices.

Guy and his brothers produced rodeos in the Pinedale and Big Piney, Wyoming, area for a time. On one occasion a man, who had entered and was bucked off, had identified himself as Guy Holt. He had a very embarrassing moment when Guy's daughter, Evelyn, was introduced to him.

Guy Holt was a gentle, quiet man, not given to "tooting his own horn" about his broncho riding abilities. His children remember him as a good cook, especially in camp. Ethel remembers his baking powder biscuits and his apple dumplings. Others remember the wonderful care he took of their mother who was severely injured once in a fall from a horse and another time when a gasoline iron exploded. He was the midwife for several of his children.

In 1926 Guy and Annie Jo moved their family to the Jackson Hole country where they ranched until bad health forced his retirement. He died in Jackson on June 26, 1946. Steamboat and Holt had each added to the other's reputation. The image of the two is a classic silhouette and a lasting legacy for the University of Wyoming Cowboys.

OSCAR HUBBARD

CHEYENNE FRONTIER DAYS 1910 was the setting for Oscar Hubbard's ride on Steamboat.

A Cheyenne newspaper described the event this way: "Hubbard was game and while the old-time favorite did not seem to have quite as much snap as he did in his younger days, he gave Hubbard two long strings of pitches going right through a crowd of moving picture men and nearly over a fence into the race track. Hubbard remained in the saddle and got recognition from the grandstands."

It's not known where Hubbard called home or what became of him after his ride on Steamboat.

ANGELO HUGHES

HUGHES RODE STEAMBOAT several times while with the Irwin Brothers Show.

FRANK IRWIN

THOUGH NOT AS WELL KNOWN as his brother C.B., Frank Irwin was a top cowboy who made a name for himself as a partner in the Irwin Brothers Wild West Show.

Some years just seem to be made for certain people, and 1902 was certainly Frank Irwin's chance to draw attention. In addition to a splendid performance in the wild horse race, he was the cowboy chosen to ride Steamboat when the black horse first appeared at Cheyenne Frontier Days.

Everyone associated with the broncho bucking contest knew the cowboy who drew Steamboat could win the world championship if he only stuck with the big horse. The honor went to Frank Irwin who was a small man weighing less than 120 pounds.

Frank's brothers, Charlie (C.B.) and Bill, held the horse while Frank cinched his saddle tight. Steamboat's feet were braced wide apart as he prepared for the first jump. Charlie and Bill pulled the blindfold off, and Steamboat exploded. The horse was "sunfishing" and "swapping ends" in an attempt to unseat the wiry rider.

Frank wasn't on long when he went off the right side of the horse, catching his foot in the stirrup where he swung for a period before being thrown free.

That same year, Frank competed in the wild horse race at Cheyenne Frontier Days. *Leslie's Weekly* described the event this way:

"The wild horse race proved to be one of the most interesting and exciting events of all. Imagine a dozen wild horses bolting through the open gates of the pen and making frantic attempts to escape the ropes of the dare-devil men endeavoring to saddle and hobble them and then ride the outlaws round the half mile track. In this exhibition one of the horses got away after being roped and a wild chase took place before he could be roped again.

"Before this wild-horse race could begin it was necessary to subdue the untamed broncs. One of the cowboys, swinging a lariat in his hand, darted into the medley of cowboys and wild horses, then came bolting out, whooping and dragging a panic-stricken cayuse at the end of his rope. This was repeated over and over again, until, on the track in front of the grandstand, there stood panting and struggling, about a dozen wild, vicious and defiant steeds, fighting unsuccessfully against their cowboy conquerors. A dozen saddles lay scattered on the ground and their riders stood ready to spring at the horse's head at the word 'go.'

"At a signal the riders started to saddle. The helpers were jerked in all directions. It was an indescribable sight; men dodging wildly back and forth, horses wild with fear or mad with rage, bounding, bucking, rearing and rolling all over the track. Out of the seething cauldron of men and beasts a horse was seen emerging, struggling and lunging for liberty, ridden by a slight but very wiry youth, Frank Irwin of Bosler, Wyoming.

"Following closely came the others, all lunging and pitching in their frantic and unsuccessful efforts to unseat their riders. The Bosler lad saddled, mounted and broke his bronco, and rode over the half mile in 1:31.4—the quickest time ever made in a wild-horse race."

JAKE MARING

LARAMIE COWBOY JAKE Maring is often credited as the model for the Wyoming license plate because of a conversation he had with Wyoming Secretary of State Lester Hunt reported in detail in Chapter Nine.

The cowboy and Hunt agreed if a license plate was designed for Wyoming depicting a rider atop a bucking broncho, the cowboy would be Maring. A photo of Maring on Steamboat was provided to Hunt for use in designing the plate. But not long after the conversation the two men had a falling out, and it was never clear whether Hunt stuck to the agreement.

Maring had his first shot at Steamboat in 1905 at the Albany County Fair where he attempted to ride the black horse in an effort to win a one hundred dollar bet. Although he used a quirt, Maring soon found that Steamboat wouldn't be whipped or scratched. After about six or eight jumps, Maring lost his seat, he once said.

Maring again rode Steamboat at a Fourth of July celebration in 1911. By then the cowboy had his nickname "Eat 'em up Jake" for he was wild, loquacious, and reckless. Each time Steamboat hit the dirt in a jarring jump, Jake Maring gave out a whoop. He said he rode Steamboat on that try "but couldn't eat for two weeks after that because of the shaking I got."

Cowboy Jake Maring grits his teeth atop Steamboat as the horse demonstrates his unique bucking style. Maring, a Laramie resident, climbed aboard Steamboat at least three times, twice in Laramie and once in Denver. He bit the dust on two of those occasions, but he may have stayed aboard on one of his Laramie rides. (Photo courtesy of Emery Miller, Laramie, Wyoming.)

At the Albany County Fair that same year Maring got another chance at Steamboat as the result of a one hundred dollar bet between Billy Owen and Charlie Irwin. Owen was sure Maring could whip and scratch Steamboat from start to finish. But when Maring mounted and said "Let him go" Steamboat took off with a snort, taking little time to dump Maring, according to newspaper reports. Once again Maring had whipped and scratched Steamboat from the start, but the horse jumped and twisted out from under him. Losing his seat was no disgrace for Maring, for many other top cowboys had met the same fate when given a shot at riding Steamboat.

"I did nothing but ride bucking horses all my life. For nine years I followed the rodeo, and I can conscientiously say Steamboat was the hardest bucking horse I was ever on. I never rode a horse that was any comparison to him as a true hard bucking horse. After riding him I was unable to eat anything for several days."

Maring was born August 14, 1884. He came to Wyoming in 1901 from Denver to work on the King and Riverside Ranches. He had a career with the Union Pacific Railroad from 1909 to 1959 serving as an engineer on such trains as the old "844" steam engine that in 1991 was still chugging its way across southern Wyoming, billowing out black smoke and reminding people of an earlier age.

Maring died December 23, 1970.

EDWARD T. MCCARTY

EDWARD TRUMBLE MCCARTY, known as Eddie, was born January 1, 1887, in Loveland, Colorado, but he grew up on a ranch near Chugwater where he broke horses and worked cattle. In 1910 he was in the wild horse race at Cheyenne Frontier Days for his first taste of rodeo competition, and in Douglas he rode Steamboat to capture his place in history. No details are available about his Steamboat ride, but it put him in a unique position in rodeo history.

McCarty was personally involved with three of the five greatest bucking horses in the history of rodeo as recognized by the National Cowboy Hall of Fame in Oklahoma City. Included in the Bucking Horse Hall of Fame are Steamboat, Midnight and Five Minutes to Midnight, horses with a McCarty connection.

McCarty is said to have started collecting rough stock for his rodeo string as early as 1912. In 1913 he and Van Guilford got the contract to furnish stock for Cheyenne Frontier Days, winning the contract away from C. B. Irwin. Steamboat was not in their "string" of bucking horses, so McCarty's entrance into the Cheyenne production was offset by Steamboat's exit. In 1917 McCarty merged operations with Verne Elliott of Platteville, Colorado, but it wasn't until 1922 that they really made a name for themselves at Tex Rickard's Rodeo in Madison Square Garden. There they staged the first indoor rodeo.

The pair produced rodeos in London, England, in 1924 and in 1934. They furnished stock for the top shows including Cheyenne Frontier Days, the Southwestern Exposition and Fat Stock Show Rodeo in Fort Worth, Texas, and the Pendleton Roundup, as well as for rodeos in Chicago and New York City.

McCarty had a good eye for "bad" horses, having ridden them himself; he was world champion in 1919. As a stock contractor he collected a select group of those outlaw horses including Midnight and Five Minutes to Midnight. Top cowboys of the day knew they had done something right if they succeeded in riding either of those horses.

Stock contractor Eddie McCarty, shown here atop Last Chance during Cheyenne Frontier Days, knew how to select bucking horses because he rode plenty of them, including Steamboat. He is one of four men to climb on Steamboat who are recognized at the National Cowboy Hall of Fame. (National Cowboy Hall of Fame and Western Heritage Center.)

Midnight is buried at the National Cowboy Hall of Fame where a tombstone reads:

1910-1936
"Under this sod lies a great bucking hoss
There never lived a cowboy he couldn't toss
His name was Midnight
His coat black as coal
If there is a hoss-heaven
Please, God, rest his soul"

A similar monument to Five Minutes to Midnight reads:

> 1924-1947
> August 1
> Again The Reaper
> Has Visited
> The Corral
> He Took
> 5 minutes to midnight
> The cowboys pal
> —A Cowboy

The Steamboat monument features a reproduction of the 1903 photo of Guy Holt by B.C. Buffum.

A contemporary of McCarty once said, "he was about half-human to cowboys, as compared to most stock contractors in those days."

McCarty won the world championship in steer wrestling in 1909 and in bull dogging in 1914. He contributed to rodeo long after he quit riding. He was inducted into the Rodeo Cowboy Hall of Fame in 1970.

McCarty married Betty Riner in 1933. He died of a heart attack on May 31, 1946.

GENE MCKAY

GENE MCKAY FAILED in an attempt on Steamboat in 1912 at the Albany County fair in Laramie.

CHARLIE MCKINLEY

IF CHARLIE MCKINLEY of Platteville, Colorado, had gotten a better performance out of Steamboat when he rode him in 1910, he might have won the world championship. Instead it went to Sam Scoville for the second time. News accounts of the 1910 ride said Steamboat had lost his punch, and he was no longer the king of the bucking horses. McKinley did win the title aboard another horse in 1911.

TOM MINOR

IDAHO COWBOY TOM Minor is the first man known to climb aboard Steamboat in a rodeo arena. He took his seat at the Festival of Mountain and Plain in Denver in 1901 and made a commendable ride even though it didn't earn him the championship buckle in a head-to-head contest with Thad Sowder.

The *St. Louis Globe Democrat* reported the contest this way: "Probably the most memorable contest was when Tom Minor of Idaho, a showy rider and one of the best ever born to the saddle, fought with Thad Sowder for the championship belt at Denver. The riders were even until the final rides, and then it was decided to give them both a try-out on the back of Steamboat. One rode the outlaw one day and the other rider tried his luck in the saddle on the following day, giving the horse the benefit of a rest between rides. Both riders were nearly thrown, but it was decided Sowder had made a trifle better ride than Minor, so the championship went to him, while Steamboat was adjudged the worst horse that had come off the plains in many a year."

Tom was a wiry rider who had busted bronchos since he was a lad in Nevada and Idaho. He was born March 3, 1871, in Steubenville, Ohio, but Minor's family moved to Nevada when he was only a year old, and he got his first livestock experience at age eleven while herding horses for the Harvey Brothers' DH Ranch, a large outfit in Paradise Valley, in Humboldt County.

In 1882 the Minor family moved to the Quinn River Valley, about twenty-five miles south of McDermitt, to raise a few head of cattle, but Tom remained with the DH for two years. His family's operation wasn't large enough to suit him, and when Tom left the DH he went over to Quinn River where he hired on for a four-year stint as a horse wrangler with the Hoppin brothers.

Working with horses daily, quickly gave him confidence that he was old enough and big enough to ride any horse on the spread. He got lots of experience on the back of the big, salty Nevada horses before he went north to Trout Creek, Oregon, where he was hired on in his first job as a full-fledged broncho rider for the Spur outfit. His boss, Mike Finn, was considered one of the best broncho riders in that state. Minor, Jim Hornback, a broncho rider from Modoc County, California, and Texas Jack were the crew.

The fall roundups were over when Minor left Oregon, to return to Elko County, Nevada. Jobs were scarce, so he started driving a mule team hauling wood and freight from Elko to the mining camp of Tuscarora.

After one trip Tom was in town when some cowpunchers just off the roundup were having some fun riding a few rank horses. The top rider bit the dust hard. Minor witnessed the exhibition, then made up his mind he could, and would, ride the horse, but for money.

The townspeople, anxious to see if the young man who was barely out of his teens could ride the horse, quickly raised a two hundred dollar purse. The amount was equal to four months of wages for Tom, and he swung into the saddle, a seat he was still in when the dust settled.

When the ride was finished, Tom not only had the two hundred dollar purse, but also a job as a broncho rider with the P-Bench, one of the large outfits in Elko County. He immediately turned his mule team over and climbed into the saddle of his new job. After nearly five years with the P-Bench, Tom went to visit his family at Quinn River where he met a New York girl whom he married in Winnemucca, Nevada, July 19, 1894.

Soon after their wedding they moved to Modoc County, California, where Tom broke colts for cow outfits at twelve dollars a head for a couple of years.

The trail finally led to Idaho where Minor made a business of handling large numbers of horses—buying, selling, and breaking them for ranch work. While engaged in this horse business, he competed in as many local contests as possible and won a good bit of prize money.

While Minor rode in many small contests in Idaho, his abilities attracted the eye of rich mining man John Cammit who saw him ride an exceptionally bad horse at Hailey, Idaho. Cammit worked to get Minor to head to Cheyenne Frontier Days, but Tom doubted he was good enough to compete so he maintained his winning pace in Idaho.

Although Minor did compete in Denver in 1901, it wasn't until 1905 that Cammitt, Dr. Jim Emerson, and Frank Winchester agreed to pay his entry fees and expenses if he would ride at Cheyenne. Figuring he had nothing to lose, Minor packed his saddle and set out for Cheyenne where he drew favorable comment, even though he didn't win the broncho riding championship.

KID MOORE

MOORE RODE STEAMBOAT October 4, 1911, in Cheyenne at a complimentary mini-show of the Irwin Brothers Cheyenne Frontier Days Wild West Show held for the visit of President William Howard Taft. No other information about Moore is known.

WILLIAM "BILLY" MURRAY

PINE BLUFFS, WYOMING, cowboy William "Billy" Murray, who lived in the Horse Creek area, rode Black Bear to get to the finals at Cheyenne Frontier Days in 1906 and was in a three-way ride-off with William Grieser and Clayton Danks for the championship when he drew Steamboat.

The horse gave an exhibition of some of the worst bucking ever seen at the park and newspaper reports said, "It is a question whether any of the riders of the park could have stuck with the veteran old outlaw yesterday and while Murray, in being thrown, lost all chance for the championship, he lost none of his fame as a rider in biting the dust under Steamboat's feet."

Grieser went on to win the title in 1906, and Danks won it in 1907 and 1909, but little mention was made of William Murray in subsequent years.

Murray was the son of William and Catherine Murray. The family lived in Cheyenne at least from 1888 until 1896, then the parents bought the Krakow Place north of Cheyenne, later known as the Donahue-Rutledge Ranch. His father was a mail carrier between Cheyenne and LaGrange from 1896 until 1898. The children in the family were Jim, Billy, Frank, Jack, Margaret, Josephine, Ann, and Catherine.

William Murray's brother, Jim Murray, also was a broncho rider, performing at Cheyenne Frontier Days in steer roping, wild horse racing, and other events.

Jim Murray, in an interview in 1974 in the *Wyoming Eagle*, said his brother, Billy, was one of the best Frontier Days broncho riders. "One year Billy had 75 points and was way ahead of three other performers in the finals. But he drew the famous bucking horse, 'Steamboat,' and met his doom. Billy got bucked off."

CRAVEL PAGUS

CRAVEL PAGUS WAS one of the top riders for the Buffalo Bill Wild West Show. One story is that he was sent by Colonel William F. Cody to ride Steamboat when Buffalo Bill made an offer of two thousand dollars to buy Steamboat. Pagus was bucked off during the ride, and Cody withdrew his offer in disgust. No other information is available about Pagus.

OTTO PLAGA

STEAMBOAT POPPED AND cracked, twisted and sunfished for more than eighty jumps before he successfully threw Otto

Plaga, a wiry man who grew up on one of the first ranches established on the Sybille between Chugwater and Bosler.

Family stories say Otto was bucked off after eighty-eight jumps, but one old-timer in the area said he only lasted eighty-six hops aboard Steamboat. That pioneer, Vic White, once said Plaga "rode the world's outstanding horse, old Steamboat, with ease any time he was sober. However, he got filled up on bad whiskey before he got on him one time and fell off after riding him eighty-six jumps and lost all the money all us boys had by doing so."

Plaga was a top cowboy who won the Cheyenne Frontier Days broncho riding championship in 1901. He gained notoriety when he was a key defense witness at Tom Horn's trial for the murder of Willie Nickell.

Otto W. Plaga was born in New York City, New York, December 31, 1877. He came to Wyoming with his parents, Ernest and Julia Barbara Keilhauer Plaga, in 1879. Ernest and Julia were the parents of several children who died while they were living in the Bowery of New York. Otto was their only surviving child when they first settled in Laramie where Ernest worked as a machinist.

In 1882 another son, Albin, was born. On July 14, 1886, the original 160 acres of the Plaga Ranch on Sybille Creek were homesteaded by Ernest, but the actual ranch work was done by Julia. She took the two boys, then ages eight and four, to Sybille to prove up on the homestead claim while Ernest continued to live and work in Laramie. When possible, he would make the horseback or buggy trip to the homestead.

Otto Plaga's early life on his family's ranch taught him dedication to complete a job, and he worked long hours doing necessary chores. When the required labor was done he found time and energy to perfect himself in riding, roping, and target shooting, with time for school as well.

Plaga chose for his friends older men with reputations for honesty and loyalty. Of medium height and weight with flashing black eyes and straight black thick hair, Plaga was ideally suited to the role of broncho buster.

Having won the broncho riding contest in Cheyenne in 1901, Otto was back at Frontier Days in 1905 where he drew Steamboat for the second day of competition. The performance became legendary as Plaga rode with effortless grace and perfect balance, while working his feet like he was riding a bicycle.

When Steamboat was let loose, Plaga immediately started to scratch him and whip him adding "fat to the fire." The horse bucked to the right and to the left, switching ends, sunfishing, and bucking close to the race track and into the borrow pit near it. When that happened Plaga was sent flying, but even as he lost his seat, he slapped Steamboat across the rump as a farewell gesture. It had taken eighty-eight jumps for the mighty black horse to unseat the wiry black-haired cowboy, family accounts and newspaper reports show.

Plaga's family says he had a "wild and wooly past." That could have included his acquaintance with Tom Horn, although the range detective, who often stopped to visit or have a meal with the Plaga family, is remembered as being particularly well-mannered and polite. The two met while they were riding the range, family stories say.

Horn's fate hinged somewhat upon the testimony of twenty-four-year-old Otto Plaga who swore under oath at the trial that on the day Willie Nickell was killed Plaga had seen the stock detective some twenty-five miles from where the shooting occurred.

Plaga testified he was gathering cattle and prospecting at the time he spotted Horn, but that he didn't talk to Horn. The prosecution witnesses said Plaga was a notorious storyteller, that he could not be believed under oath, and that his reputation for truth and veracity were very bad. Prosecutors successfully tore apart Plaga's testimony even though it was corroborated by another Sybille rancher who had discussed the killing with Plaga.

The defense presented its own lineup of witnesses including Sam Moore, manager of the Swan Land and Cattle Company, and Duncan Clark manager of John Coble's Iron Mountain Ranch, who both said Plaga's reputation for telling the truth was good. Nevertheless, Plaga's testimony concerning Horn's whereabouts the day of the Nickell killing wasn't enough to acquit the accused man.

Riding bronchos was a pleasure of his youth, and from November 1910 until May 1914 Plaga served as a secret service man in Mexico. Then he resigned to accept a position as Special Agent for the Southern Pacific Railway Company, which he held from May 1914 to October 1918.

Plaga returned to Wheatland, Wyoming, in 1919 and was hired as marshal in June. During that three-year term, a number of robberies were reported. Finally suspicion fastened on T. W. Cooper, night operator for the Colorado and Southern Railway. Cooper had free access to the areas where the stolen items were located. When Plaga learned Cooper was peddling goods about town, he decided to arrest him on a charge of selling goods without a license, but first Plaga watched Cooper a few days and discovered him overcharging passengers for their tickets.

Other problems cropped up including shortages in cash drawers at the railroad and missing items from an express car. Before Plaga had adequate proof to make a charge of burglary against Cooper, the suspect was relieved of his duties and prepared to leave town. Plaga arrested him on the charge of peddling without a license and placed Cooper in jail.

After the arrest, Plaga and the sheriff searched Cooper's rooms and the freight room at the depot, where they found nearly two thousand dollars worth of stolen goods. Cooper, who was twenty-four, cited his youth combined with an illness while in the Army as making him irresponsible. He was found guilty and received a sentence of not more than ten years in the State Industrial School in Worland.

Plaga was a sleuth and solved the Banner Grocery robbery in Wheatland where the only clue was that of the print of a high-heeled boot under one window. Plaga remembered seeing a pair of boot soles of the same type on a bench at the waiting room of the depot and upon this thread of evidence achieved the arrest and conviction of Henry Tatum.

Plaga left the Wheatland marshal position in 1922 to return to work as a Special Agent for the Colorado and Southern Railway Company. He was there until March 1923 when he again resigned to accept a position as Federal Prohibition and Revenue Officer, which he held from March 1923 to September 1926.

Plaga was injured as a prohibition officer when he was assisting in destroying a still and contents on a ranch some twelve miles east of Casper on December 4, 1923. The place was soaked in gasoline which exploded when a lighted sack was thrown into the area. Plaga was thrown high into the air along with timber and debris, but he escaped with a gash on his head, cuts about his face, and a sprained ankle.

During Prohibition, Plaga won an enviable reputation. From March 23, 1923, to October 31, 1925, he arrested 283 people for liquor violations, seized 138 stills, 1,208 gallons of whiskey, two five-ton trucks, three automobiles, ten guns and fifteen hundred one-gallon glass jugs. He also destroyed 6,745 gallons of mash, 4,026 bottles of beer, 735 gallons of wine, eight hundred fifty-gallon barrels of mash, 3,350 twenty-gallon barrels of whiskey and six hundred ten-gallon whiskey kegs.

Plaga worked for the Union Pacific Railroad in Cheyenne and Green River from 1926 until 1928.

On March 31, 1928, Plaga married Carol Jeanne Knudson of Sturgeon, Wisconsin. It was his second marriage. His first was to a woman whose name has dropped into oblivion. Otto and Carol had one son, Otto Jr., who died in infancy. The couple moved to Carbon County that year, where Otto worked as a deputy sheriff in Rawlins, Wyoming, for three years.

Work as a peace officer cost Plaga his hand in Rawlins, during a riot at the state penitentiary. He was guarding the one hundred prisoners alone when the trouble started. A disturbance in the jail kitchen caused Plaga to rush in, but when he did, the prisoners attacked him. One of the inmates was armed with a big, sharp butcher knife and another with a hammer. As the prisoner with the knife lunged forward, Plaga struck the man in the mouth. The prisoner had snaggled prominent teeth that made a jagged surface, and the hardness of the blow drove one of the broken teeth into Plaga's hand between the first and second fingers of his right hand. The man with the hammer was poised for a blow when Plaga drove his already injured hand against the prisoner's face, lacerating the hand still further.

Three of the prisoners escaped, but Plaga started after them when dawn broke. He recaptured two of them fairly quickly and later arrested the third escapee. But when Plaga went to Rawlins to have his sore hand examined, the doctor found the jagged tooth of the convict had penetrated the bone, and blood poisoning of the marrow had set in. It was necessary to amputate the hand at the wrist.

In 1931, Plaga and his wife moved to Saratoga where they ran a bath house for five years. Finally, in September 1936,

Plaga returned to Wheatland to take a job as Platte County Deputy Sheriff. In 1946 Plaga was appointed as Justice of the Peace in Wheatland, a position he held until his death.

Although an accomplished broncho rider, Otto was mainly involved in law enforcement. He did a limited amount of mining and exploration and didn't continue his involvement with the family ranch. That fell to Albin who eventually raised commercial Hereford cattle. On January 8, 1908, Albin married Mary Irene McComber at the McComber home in Wheatland. They worked the ranch which remained in the Plaga family until 1988, most recently operated by their grandson, Greg Garton.

It's ironic that the man whose testimony about Tom Horn was not believed, later became a distinguished law enforcement officer and justice of the peace—and that the hand Plaga used to grip the hackamore rope when he rode Steamboat was later amputated.

BOWMAN RILEY

RILEY, AN EMPLOYEE of the Irwin brothers, rode Steamboat in Salt Lake City in 1910. He was from Laramie originally.

SAM SCOVILLE

ONE OF THE TOP RIDERS of the Steamboat era was Cheyenne cowboy Sam Scoville who won two world championship titles, the first in 1905 when he tied with Hugh Clark and the second in 1910 when he edged past Charlie McKinley to win.

To tie for top honors in 1905 at Cheyenne, Scoville, who worked on the Tom O'Neil Ranch, rode Steamboat. "Scoville rode the outlaw to a standstill, quirting him at every jump and incidentally won a side bet of one hundred dollars that he could scratch the animal during his ride," the *Wyoming Semi-Weekly Tribune* reported.

In 1908 Scoville was unlucky in drawing Black Cat at Cheyenne Frontier Days. The horse was described as a "regular spittin' kitten" who fought against being saddled until he was too tired to put up much of a show in the bucking contest. Scoville was given another horse to ride, Horse Creek, but that mount also failed to perform to the best of his ability and didn't do much bucking until after Scoville was off. Then Horse Creek decided it was fairly important to get that saddle off his back, and he put on quite a show without the rider.

The year of his second world championship, 1910, Scoville drew Teddy Roosevelt in a good contest. The horse was described as the hardest jumper of the day who "sunfished, whirled, twisted and tried to tie knots with his legs at every jump, but the plucky rider waved his hat in the air and showed the crowd that even Teddy could not get the best of him."

Scoville's second world championship title might not have been his if Steamboat had bucked with the strength and style he had in earlier years. For the contest Charles McKinley drew Steamboat but placed second. If Steamboat had only given McKinley a little shaking, the results might have been different, a newspaper account of the contest said.

In an exhibition that same year Scoville gave a thrilling ride on an unnamed wild horse. He did so without a saddle or bridle, but by holding onto a rope which was tied about the animal's body. The horse pitched for some distance and then started at a two minute clip around the race track. All the rider could do was to hang on during the race until another cowboy overtook the horse. Scoville made a change onto the back of the other horse while both animals were going at full speed.

Following that wild ride Scoville once more thrilled his admirers by riding a wild steer without a saddle, and the bovine put on a very good exhibition of pitching.

Though Scoville was a Cheyenne cowboy little other detail is known about his life.

CARL SMITH

BLACK COWBOY CARL Smith got his chance aboard Steamboat in the fall of 1907 in Fort Collins, Colorado, but the horse had the man beaten before he even climbed aboard.

Smith regarded the horse as "black death" but wouldn't withdraw from the contest when he knew he had drawn Steamboat as his mount. Carl was nervous as he mounted and settled himself securely in the saddle seat. Taking his grip on the hackamore reins, Smith whispered, "Let him go."

Nobody needed to tell Steamboat what to do. He was all wound up to explode and unwind. Carl Smith was not aboard when the horse completed his opening moves.

MARTIN "THAD" SOWDER

THE FIRST WORLD champion broncho buster shook the hand of the King of England and U.S. President Teddy Roosevelt, he rode the hurricane deck of the wildest bucking horses, including Steamboat, at the turn of the century, and he had his own wild west show. But Martin T. "Thad" Sowder paid the price for his prowess atop a horse, in later years suffering from paralysis resulting from a hard fall onto his head when he was only sixteen.

Only three names are listed on the Denver Festival of Mountain and Plain silver belt, and two of them are Thad Sowder. He claimed that title in 1901 and 1902, but the belt had to be won by the same cowboy three times in order for him to keep permanent possession. Sowder didn't ride for the belt in 1903, and the honor went to Guy Holt. Sponsors of the belt never offered it in a contest again.

Although Sowder never claimed the belt permanently, his name is etched on it, and his mark is in history because of his ability on the back of a pitching horse.

Sowder was born January 19, 1874, in Pulaksi County, Kentucky, the seventh child of David and Martha Sowder, and moved to Iowa with his family when he was nine years old. His father died shortly afterward and his mother moved west to Julesburg, Colorado, with her children where she purchased a ranch from her daughter and son-in-law about twenty miles from town. Not long after Sowder became a teenager, he decided to ride every horse on the ranch his mother christened the Lazy D.

This decision would change his life when one pitching cayuse threw him onto his head fracturing his skull. But Sowder, then sixteen, was not easily defeated and, after he had patched himself up a bit, he got back on the outlaw horse and rode him to a finish.

Sowder's first job as a cowboy was on his mother's Lazy D Ranch and there he received his schooling on how to stay in the saddle of a bucking, sunfishing, twisting horse.

By 1897 Sowder was ready to throw his hat in the ring with the other cowboys of the area and surprised everyone at the Cheyenne Frontier Day when he rode High Five, who was said to be the worst horse in the show.

Then Sowder took a job breaking horses for Theodore Roosevelt's Rough Riders, but, in 1898, he was back in Cheyenne where he topped Royal Flush.

There was no official world championship for broncho riding prior to 1902. But in 1901 J.M. Kuykendall awarded a five hundred dollar silver belt set with a large ruby as the first championship belt for broncho riders.

Sowder was working for the Diamond Ranch near Gillette, Wyoming, when he saw a circular about the Kuykendall belt. He decided to try to win that prize.

So at the Festival of Mountain and Plain in 1901, Thad Sowder rode horses called Peggy and Steamboat, winning the Kuykendall belt and with it the right to call himself Champion Broncho Rider of the World. Before being named champion, he'd had a ride-off with Idaho cowboy Tom Minor for the title belt. Both men rode Steamboat in the contest [*see section on Tom Minor in this chapter*]. Shortly after his win Sowder joined Buffalo Bill's Wild West Show at New York's Madison Square Garden. But he was back in Denver in August of 1902 to defend his title which he did successfully by riding both Steamboat and E.A. against William McNeerlen who had challenged him to ride for the championship belt and a bet of one thousand dollars. Although the cowboys rode under rules of the Festival of Mountain and Plain, the contest for the belt was not recognized by that association.

In 1903 the directors of the Denver Festival of Mountain and Plain agreed to have the championship belt for the rough riders' contest decided at the Cheyenne Frontier Days celebration. The decision meant "Cheyenne will have in name

Colorado cowboy Thad Sowder was the first World Champion Cowboy, named at the 1901 Festival of Mountain and Plain in Denver. For that contest Sowder rode Steamboat and Peggy. The following year he won the title and the Kuykendall belt a second time. That belt had to be won by the same cowboy three times for him to retain it, and Sowder did not compete for it again. (National Cowboy Hall of Fame and Western Heritage Center.)

what she has always had in fact, the only event where the real broncho busting championship can be decided," the *Wyoming Tribune* reported.

Because the belt had to be won three times by the same rider before it could be permanently claimed, having its ownership decided at the Frontier Days celebration meant top riders from throughout the West would participate in that show.

August 27, 1903, seven top cowboys rode for the championship and the chance to have his name engraved on the belt. Thad Sowder did not defend his title. When the dust settled from his ride on Young Steamboat, Guy Holt was declared the champion [*see section on Guy Holt in this chapter*].

Although there was some speculation that Sowder refused to defend his title for fear he would lose, he said the festival committee knew thirty days before the contest that he would not participate. He was forced to remain with his own show, which was a wild west show called Sowder's Broncho Busters, started in June of that year.

Stories that Sowder challenged Holt to a contest for the belt immediately after the Frontier Days celebration also were false. Sowder said he did challenge Holt to a competition, but it was for a wager. "The challenge is still open," he said shortly after the Frontier Days contest.

Sowder was a "yep" and "nope" cowboy who remained quietly in the background when other cowboys expounded about the rank horses they had ridden, the injuries they'd survived or the riding contests they'd won.

Sowder's wild west show was organized in June of 1903 and included top cowboys from the Wyoming plains including J. G. Wright, of Douglas, who discovered and trained the famous horse Ragalong. That mount was given to President Theodore Roosevelt when the president visited Cheyenne in 1903. The horse's name was later changed to Wyoming.

For the show, Sowder rounded up thirty of the worst horses on the plains. He took the horses and his rough riders on tour through Nebraska, Iowa, Illinois, Indiana, Ohio, and Pennsylvania. The men and horses traveled overland using a mess and camp wagon in which the men made their home as they participated in the show.

In 1905 President Roosevelt was again in Cheyenne as a spectator when Sowder made his last ride in the rodeo arena. Following Sowder's performance, the president stepped forward to shake the broncho buster's hand. But shortly after the ride, the injury Sowder had received as a sixteen-year-old rookie broncho rider came back to haunt him when he became partially paralyzed. He never rode an outlaw again.

In 1913 Sowder had surgery to remove a bone fragment from his brain, and that operation kept him from being a virtual cripple, but even so, in his later years he had frequently recurring attacks of paralysis. Consequently, the man whose name once was adequate to pack the largest arena with fans wanting to see a champion perform, led a lonely existence.

Sowder married Anna Farrell, the daughter of Mr. and Mrs. William Farrell, wealthy ranchers living north of Cheyenne. The Farrells didn't cotton to Sowder because they felt a rodeo performer was not good enough for their daughter. The courtship was rocky, and the young couple took matters into their own hands when they eloped.

Thad and Anna had two sons, Harold and Oliver. The latter died when he was only six. For a time Sowder and his family lived in Saratoga, Wyoming, where he was manager of the Hugus ranch. It was incongruous and somewhat disillusioning to see Sowder astraddle a common stool as he consumed an ice cream soda in the drugstore, back of which was the doctor's office, the early-day doctor's son, Garrett Price once recalled.

"I can't do much for him" the doctor said. "He's all busted up inside." It was true of most broncho riders. A rupture was only one of the injuries they could sustain from the violent jerking to which their bodies were subjected.

The marriage to Anna was ill-fated, and she left Sowder to remarry. Later when she and her second husband were found dead in a lonely Wyoming cabin, suspicion for the murders immediately centered on Thad Sowder. However, he was in Denver at the time of the deaths and had a perfect alibi. So far as is known, the crime never was solved.

Sowder died in March 1931 at the old home of the family in Julesburg. His obituary said during Sowder's later years "he became a habitue of the loafing places of Julesburg's main street and sometimes between attacks of paralysis [went] to Denver for the National Western Livestock Show or to Cheyenne for Frontier Days. When he did he could always be found watching with wistful eyes the corrals of the bucking horses."

No doubt Thad Sowder was recalling the pitching and twisting bronchos he had conquered.

DICK STANLEY

A mystery man of the Steamboat era was Dick Stanley. Or was he? Stanley arrived in Cheyenne in 1908 togged out in fringed buckskins, wearing a mustache, and Buffalo Bill-style goatee. He attracted much attention. Stanley was there for the annual Frontier Days Celebration.

New steel grandstands had replaced the old wooden ones and electric street cars took people to the new grounds. Trick riding, horse racing and steer roping were parts of the rodeo, but mostly the spectators wanted to see the broncho riding.

Broncho riding was the glamour event. Everyone had a favorite among the cowboys. It was unusual to have a rider come from far away, so it's not surprising that the attention of the crowd came to rest on Dick Stanley.

Stanley qualified for the finals by riding Fighting Sam. He had arrived at the arena just as the bucking contest was beginning and barely had time to unpack his saddle and put on his chaps. Stanley attempted no fancy tricks, but stuck tight and rode the horse clean and straight.

That put him in the finals where he was to ride Steamboat. Conditions did not break well for Steamboat that day, because just before the ride, there was a downpour that made the ground slippery and soft. Stanley had his ride planned. He knew the horse would be handicapped because the ground would engulf his feet up to his ankles with every jump.

Stanley rode old Steamboat spurring constantly in the preliminary round, but when a furor arose about whether he had taken advantage of the horse, a ride-off with Clayton Danks was ordered. In the preliminary round Danks rode Red Bird, and for the final round Danks drew Young Steamboat while Stanley drew Beaver. When the dust finally settled, Stanley was declared the winner and world champion broncho rider.

Stanley never got another chance to ride Steamboat to prove whether he could stay aboard the black gelding in a dry arena. Stanley returned to Frontier Days in 1909, but he did not draw Steamboat. The crowds were disappointed, but the Steamboat ride went to Clayton Danks, who rode him to his second world championship. Once again the charge was leveled that Steamboat was not the horse of his earlier days— that his years in the arena were catching up to him.

Who was this mystery man who had come to ride the great Steamboat in 1908? Dick Stanley was not exactly a stranger to Wyoming, and maybe if the lawmen had looked a bit closer, they might have found the face of an escaped outlaw. Newspapers gave Stanley's age as twenty-eight, but that, like his name, was a sham. It's most likely he was really Earl Shobe who had come to Wyoming in 1902 straight from a stint with the Pawnee Bill Wild West Show. He was outfitted in an assortment of cowboy regalia including a pair of pearl handled .44 Remington pistols. With Shobe were a wild Oklahoman and a man called John Frederick, who later turned out to be his brother. They found work on the Laurel Leafe Ranch some fifty miles south of Buffalo on the North Fork of the Powder River. Shobe worked as a rider and the other two were ranchhands.

It was soon apparent, however, that Shobe was a horse fighter, and he was often dumped by the mean horses on the ranch. He was generally restricted to riding the spoiled horses, and when he used a good saddle horse which he didn't appreciate, Shobe was fired from his riding job.

Most agree the name Shobe was an alias, that his real name was Stanley Dickinson. Later Shobe became involved with Butch Cassidy's "Hole in the Wall Gang" and ran stolen horses from South Dakota. He is said to have robbed the post office in Buffalo in 1903 along with Jim McCloud. The two used unshod horses, then later changed to horses wearing shoes. They were eventually tracked by a posse and, following a shooting fray, Shobe escaped to Bear Trap Canyon where he recovered from wounds received in the shooting before heading west to California.

McCloud was arrested and placed in the Cheyenne jail where he attempted an escape with Tom Horn who was scheduled to hang soon for the murder of Willie Nickell [*see*

Chapter Four]. Both McCloud and Horn were recaptured, but Shobe was never heard from again — at least by that name.

With Shobe's escape after the Buffalo robbery, rumors flew. He had bragged of killing a Chicago policeman and a Wyoming sheepherder, and some said his boasts were just that, the talk of a braggart, while others believed them to be true exploits.

In any case, Shobe disappeared to reappear, some believe, as Dick Stanley several years later. He organized "Dick Stanley's Wild West Show" on the West Coast and tried to capitalize on his reputation as "the man who rode Steamboat."

Ironically, he died in October of 1910 when a broncho fell on him while he was doing a dare-devil feat on horseback at Cerea, California. The *Denver Post* reported the man Dick Stanley was "none other than Earl Shobo, wanted and diligently searched for by detectives of the Wyoming Woolgrowers Association in connection with the murder of Ben Minnick on the Minnick sheep ranch near Thermopolis eight years ago." He went by several aliases including Dick Stanley, Stanley Dickensen, Earl Shobe, but the *Denver Post* reported he was buried by relatives in Urbana, Illinois, in 1910 under the name Earl Shobo.

BENJAMIN F. STONE

BENJAMIN FRANKLIN (Frank) Stone drifted into Wyoming in 1897 helping with a herd of cattle for E.J. Bell. He was born April 1, 1869, in Pueblo, Colorado, and went to Walla Walla, Washington, with his parents when he was eighteen years old. Stone served as a Spanish interpreter in the courts of Nevada, but his real interest was cattle and horses. He quit the interpreter work and started riding for ranches in the Fort Collins and Greeley areas.

After coming to Wyoming, Stone worked as foreman of Bell's Millbrook Ranch and also went to work for Sam Moore, foreman of the Two Bar, one of the large holdings of the Swan Land and Cattle Company. Because of his love of horses and ability to stay atop a pitching horse, his friends called him "Old Iron Horse."

In 1898 Stone married Mary Howell at the Howell Ranch home near Mountain Home, Wyoming, and they had three children, a son, Earl, and daughters, Edna and Gladys. Stone's life as a cowboy continued after his marriage.

While Stone was working at the Two Bar, Steamboat was brought into the corral to be broken as a saddle horse. He couldn't be mastered and was constantly rejected by the cowboys. That disgusted the bronc busters, Stone once said, and they sold the horse for fifty dollars to John Coble. But the price is open to speculation since some accounts say Coble bought Steamboat for twenty-five. Stone could have tried to ride Steamboat at the Two Bar, but this is not documented.

Stone's first ride on Steamboat in the rodeo arena took place at the 1902 Festival of Mountain and Plain in Denver. He also rode Steamboat at a miniature rodeo in Laramie at the stockyards. Many cowboys made the effort to subdue Steamboat that day, and Stone stayed on the longest.

Stone again rode Steamboat at the Laramie County Fairgrounds in November 1903 at a show put on by an organization known as the Cowboys and Cowgirls of the Laramie Plains. The ground was covered with snow and was slippery, making it hard for Steamboat to perform. After he had bucked across the arena, he put in four or five of the hardest jumps imaginable. To stay aboard, Stone pulled on the hackamore rope with both hands, one on each side of the pommel.

Earlier that year Stone had a slight brush with the law when he got a little too anxious during the ladies' race at the Albany County Fair in September. Charges were filed against the cowboy for "violent actions, rude behavior and unlawfully interrupting and disturbing the peace of the community in this state and of the inhabitants thereof."

The charges were sought by John Ernest, marshal at the fairgrounds during the races, and came about because Stone trespassed onto the race track during the ladies' race. The charges were filed because several people thought Stone got onto the track to stop the leading horse in the race or to assist the second horse, which he owned, and that his action jeopardized the lives of the horseback riders in the race.

But when people were questioned about the matter they agreed they had formed the wrong opinion of Stone's action, and that while he had become thoughtless during the race, he had no evil intent.

The charges were dropped when Judge Grant lectured Stone "upon the extreme danger and folly of his action." Stone was probably already aware of that danger and folly since he was knocked down and stunned by the horse in third place in the race.

Stone remembered or was a part of many interesting historical events, one being a ride with Tom Horn, whom he recalled as good company, but terribly inclined to boast of his bad deeds. Stone was with Horn on Horn's last ride as a free man. On that day Horn told Stone he had fifty-two notches on his gun and that the only killing he regretted was that of the Nickell boy.

Stone died in Laramie, September 13, 1944. He is remembered as a man who loved horses. "That was his life," his family said upon his death.

WILLIAM "BILL" TAPPAN

All his life William "Bill" Tappan was a cowboy. Born March 3, 1881, in Lake City, Iowa, to Martha and James Stanley Tappan, he came west with his family when he was seventeen. The covered wagon journey was difficult with the family members suffering from both cold and scanty provisions. They burned buffalo chips for fuel and saw the last of the wild buffalo on the plains. They knew what it was like to be followed by wolves and surrounded by lions in the woods.

After the arduous journey, the family finally arrived in Guernsey, Colorado, where Bill remained for several years before heading north to North Park, Colorado, where he filed on homestead land in 1904 when he was twenty-three.

A top rider, Bill was associated with the Buffalo Bill Wild West Show and with Charlie Irwin. A photo of him atop Steamboat was one of his prized possessions, but his family doesn't know when or where the photograph was taken. Tappan punched cows and trailed horses from Laramie to Lander, and through Nebraska, Colorado, and Wyoming.

By the time Bill was thirty-five, he had moved north again to Encampment, Wyoming, where he bought a ranch. On May 6, 1936, Bill married Clara Merrill in Burley, Idaho. They ranched in Encampment until 1959 then moved to Fort Collins for a time. In 1964 they returned to Wyoming to make their home in Saratoga until his death in 1968.

HARRY WALTERS

HARRY WALTERS, WORLD champion in 1915, is believed to have ridden Steamboat, but details on the ride aren't known.

P. J. WALTERS

P. J. WALTERS RODE STEAMBOAT on the race track at the Cheyenne Frontier Days celebration in 1911.

HARRY E. WEBB

HARRY E. WEBB RELIVED his days as a cowboy and wild west show star by writing about them in the pulp magazines that chronicled the lives and times of western men. Webb worked on ranches in Wyoming, rode with several wild west shows including the Buffalo Bill Wild West Show and the Irwin Brothers Wild West Show, where he mounted Steamboat, and worked as a cowboy movie stuntman and actor.

Webb was born in New Castle, Colorado, in 1888. Harry's mother was a tall ex-school teacher from Iowa and his father, whom he always referred to as "The Old Man," was a miner. Webb, had a brother, Charley, who was two years older, and apparently other sisters and brothers.

In New Castle Harry's father worked in coal mines. Then he got the itch for land of his own. "It was a glorious day when our wagon rolled out of that town for Meeker where the old man said he'd heard that there was good homestead land on the White River," Webb wrote in the *Westerner* in 1971.

Not long after arriving in the Meeker, Colorado, area Charley and Harry saw a couple of cowhands all decked out with good saddles and spurs. Then and there the two Webb boys vowed one day they would be cowboys.

The family homesteaded at Steamboat Springs, Colorado. Charley eventually took off, headed north to Wyoming, and soon after, Harry followed him. Harry, at age fifteen, took one of the family horses and struck out bareback for Rawlins. On the way he joined a band of gypsies, with whom he traveled for a time. He traded his bareback horse to the gypsies for a bay with a saddle. It was a poor exchange, Harry soon found, as he rode toward Rawlins. The new mount had gotten some larkspur, also known as loco weed, and had fits of falling to the ground. Harry finally reached Rawlins where he swapped horses again in a deal with the livery stable owner. The trade included a new horse, five dollars, and a weather-beaten Stetson.

With his new rig Harry said, "I could already feel the romance that Wyoming held out for me." He mounted and found himself in a saddle fight with the new horse. The dismount was not pretty as Harry landed in the dirt. But he picked himself up and headed toward Lander where Charley was working.

Upon arriving in Lander he found Charley had moved on, so in order to survive that first winter, Harry did whatever he could. He washed whiskey bottles in saloons, helped at the livery stable, and got acquainted with cowboys and bronc riders.

Those Lander cowboys would round up Indian horses from the Shoshone reservation and practice riding them. The harder they bucked, the better the cowboys liked them. It was on those Indian horses that Webb learned to stay aboard a bucking broncho. The life of a cowboy was still glamour to Harry. He wanted a riding job, but knew he needed an outfit, so he took a job digging ditches to earn a stake. With the money he earned, Harry bought at swell-fork saddle made at the state penitentiary in Rawlins, a dandy gelding with a hackamore, and a pair of cross ell spurs. It cost him fifty dollars.

About that time Webb heard of some Scottish ranchers, the Dickie Brothers, up near Meeteetse, Wyoming, who were looking for somebody to break horses. Harry headed out, but when he checked out the job, he didn't like the circumstances, so he went to work for Colonel Jay L. Torrey and George Pennoyer of the M Bar Ranch on Owl Creek instead.

One day in 1909 he was in Cody, Wyoming, when he met Buffalo Bill. The story reported in the *Denver Post* goes this way: "After loading a train with cattle one day in 1909 just outside Cody, Wyoming, a ranchhand declared that the last one to town would have to buy drinks, so the group lit out for the saloon. Webb was riding a skittery horse that once was bitten by a rattlesnake. When the group reached the center of town, Webb's horse pulled up in front of some bailing wire that had been thrown into the street from the livery stable. The horse's feet tangled in the wire, and being nervous from having been bitten by a rattlesnake not long before, he bucked across the street, up the sidewalk, and right through a drugstore window."

The whole town came running down the street to see what had happened, while the druggist applied medicine to Webb's neck and head. Among the crowd of onlookers was Buffalo Bill.

"Not a bad ride, young gobbler, for as long as it lasted," Cody is remembered to have said. He then handed Webb a business card and told him to write Johnny Baker in New York for a contract to join the Buffalo Bill Wild West Show.

Webb and his best friend, George "Gaspipe" Mullison, wrote for the contract that had some fifty clauses where riders could be dismissed without pay. The cowboys weren't to get drunk, ogle girls, use bad language or refuse to ride any horse assigned to them.

Webb and Gaspipe liked the pay, sixty dollars a month as compared with forty dollars a month at the M Bar, and took the jobs with Cody's entourage. Besides Webb, two of his brothers, apparently Charley and Gerald, worked with the Buffalo Bill show.

Webb and the other cowboys in the Buffalo Bill show would often get Colonel Cody to give them complimentary tickets which they could give to people, mostly girls, they met while performing. Once in New York, Harry got a ticket for Jane, a girl with whom he was particularly taken. He wanted to impress her with his riding ability and asked to be allowed to ride Two Step, one of the top bucking horses in the show. Webb's efforts to impress fell short when he did a belly landing on the arena floor after flying over Two Step's head. But he got the girl anyway. They later were married.

Webb rode for Buffalo Bill two years, traveling more than forty-two thousand miles and visiting thirty-one states. Webb was a strong admirer of Cody and served as the showman's valet for a time.

In 1912 Webb left the wild west show to begin working for a Pennsylvania film company. He worked for the Lubin Motion Picture Company as a cowboy actor and stuntman. His first acting job was filmed on the Delaware River. He portrayed a breech-clouted Indian and made thirty-five dollars per week. He was an extra and a stuntman in a number of movies made by Lubin and did some acting as well in movies such as *Battle of Shiloh*. He spent much of his time breaking horses for the movies. It was on a movie set that he became reacquainted with Art Acord, another Steamboat rider. Both had been with the Buffalo Bill Show in 1911. Later both also worked for the Hat Ranch in Nevada, and Webb wrote for western magazines about Acord's life as a silent movie star.

It was from Lubin that Harry Webb got his first opportunity as a writer when he was asked to compile a weekly column about what was happening at the Lubin Company western town located near Mary's Landing, New Jersey.

When Harry wrote a story about some of the problems associated with the company and the motion pictures it was making, he lost his job. "I stuck to facts a bit too well and my last contribution was also the last of our western company. My literary efforts got us all fired," Webb wrote in the *Westerner* in 1971.

Webb had perfected his roping by 1912 and worked for a couple of years with Bill Arthur at a theater chain doing trick roping. He also rode with the Irwin Brothers Wild West show in 1912 where he climbed aboard Steamboat.

In 1913 Webb signed a contract with the 101 Ranch Show touring South America, but just before he was supposed to set sail he got word that the stock had glanders and the animals had to be destroyed. It was always a good idea to have an extra contract in the pocket for just such an occasion.

In 1914 Webb and his wife signed contracts with the Miller Brothers 101 Ranch Show, Worth Brothers Wild West Show, California Frank's Wild West Show, and Wyoming Bill's Wild West Show. Webb said many performers juggled contracts by signing many, then choosing the best, and writing a note to the other shows saying they couldn't participate. The practice was not exactly on the up and up. However, bronc riders and trick ropers were a dime a dozen, so no real problems arose when one broke a contract.

Webb chose to work for the Wyoming Bill Wild West Show because its itinerary would take him back to Wyoming. Once there, Webb spent most of 1915 breaking war horses for

Bentley and Cooley at Sheridan, before heading to Nevada where he ran mustangs, hunted predators for the U.S. Biological Survey, and played the banjo or fiddle for country dances. Webb homesteaded at Pine Mountain near Elko, Nevada. He first gathered, broke, and sold wild mustangs, then he started raising cattle.

Webb was in Nevada running his ranch in 1922 when he started freelancing western stories to magazines, writing about his life, and the characters he had known. His first story was one about trapping bobcats, which could have come from his experience as a government trapper in Nevada. Though Webb didn't begin writing steadily until the 1950s, when he was in his seventies, he did periodically sell a story during the preceding thirty-year period.

Through the years he wrote, under his own name and the pseudonym Edgar Webb, such stories as "The Legend of Jim Novell," "When Horse Sense was Enough, the Jokes and Sorrows of Growin' Up in the West," "Gunfighters I Have Known," "Blood Ran on the Crowheart Butte," "The Evils of Cowboy Money," and "The Milt Hinkle Nobody Knew."

One story, "The Satan Horse" in the *Westerner* in 1974, recalled a bout Webb had with a horse in Colorado. The story made reference to Steamboat. The Colorado horse's owner said the black "satan horse" was a real "wampus cat." If that was so, Webb figured he could take him and make wages "just entering him in bucking contests same as old Steamboat was bringing in the sheckles for his owner. Hell, I couldn't lose."

Webb wrote at least until the mid-1970s for such western publications as *The West, Real West, Old Trails, Frontier Times*, and the *Westerner*. He was a contributing editor for the *Westerner*. One of his articles "Tenderfoot Cowboy" in the *Westerner* was the story of Georgie Farnsworth, a kid Harry's son brought home one day when they lived in

Nevada. The story was turned into a book, *A Boy Called Nothin*, and made into a movie by Walt Disney. During his career he wrote 116 stories and only two were rejected.

In 1972, a full fifty years after he started writing for western magazines, Harry Webb won the top award, the Golden Spur, given by the Western Writers of America for his non-fiction article "Call of the Cow Country" which appeared in the *Westerner* in three parts.

The story started, "From the time I was eight years old, Wyoming had been my lode-star and as the years dragged, its pull had grown even stronger." Harry Webb then went on to tell the true story of his life as a cowboy, broncho buster, and wild west star. He died in 1984 at age ninety-six.

BIBLIOGRAPHY

PART ONE

CHAPTER ONE

THIS BOOK STARTED AT the suggestion of Cody artist Peter M. Fillerup, who had been commissioned to do a larger-than-life- size monument to Steamboat for the University of Wyoming to commemorate Wyoming's Centennial. Information about his sculpture is from personal interviews conducted by Candy Moulton in 1989 and 1990.

The newspapers of the period from 1897 to 1915 published in Cheyenne, Denver, and Laramie provided the background for this chapter.

The information about Guy Holt's ride on Steamboat in 1903 is from articles in the *Laramie Boomerang* and "Steamboat—King of the Buckers!" by Sam Howe, which appeared in *Western Horseman*, July 1954, while Holt's connection with the University of Wyoming logo comes from family documents and *Steamboat, Symbol of Wyoming Spirit* by A.S. "Bud" Gillespie and R.H. "Bob" Burns (University of Wyoming, 1952) which was an invaluable reference source for much of this book. Flossie Moulton has a personal copy of that publication which belonged to her mother, Gwen Holt Woodward, but others were made available to us at the American Heritage Center and Wyoming State Archives. David Roberts, student publications director for the University of Wyoming, made a copy of the publication for us, and Andy Hysong of Laramie provided an original copy.

We used that document as a starting point for our story, by compiling a list of cowboys Burns and Gillespie said had ridden Steamboat. We must note, however, that in our search we could not document at least two of the cowboy rides Burns and Gillespie reported; therefore, we have not included those stories in this book. We believe other cowboys may have ridden Steamboat and invite anyone with documentation of rides to contact us.

One of the first treasures we found was Jimmy Danks's account of his ride on Steamboat and of his naming of the horse. That document is located at the Wyoming State Archives. Danks's information also gave us detail about Steamboat's breeding.

The first we knew of another Wyoming horse used as an emblem was when an employee at UW's American Heritage Center told us about a restricted file there that told the story of Ostrom's horse. Further inquiry led to the unpublished manuscript, "The Beginning of a Great Emblem" by George N. Ostrom at the Wyoming State Archives and to a document prepared by the Archives for the Wyoming Centennial. Information about the history of the Wyoming license plate was found in a publication at the Saratoga Historical and Cultural Association Museum in Saratoga.

CHAPTER TWO

MUCH OF THE INFORMATION for this chapter came from Jimmy Danks's recollections, cited earlier. As mentioned, *Steamboat, Symbol of Wyoming Spirit* by Gillespie and Burns was a great help to us. It was written at a time when the University of Wyoming first considered erecting a monument to Steamboat in Prexy's Pasture. Burns and Gillespie had the advantage of working in an earlier time period which allowed them to personally contact many of the cowboys who had ridden Steamboat in competition. Though the statue was never made, partly due to financial reasons and partly because university officials had difficulty in determining which end of the campus would view Steamboat's head and which his rear end, the book was published with personal recollections by Gillespie, who was a handler of the horse for many years. Burns, a UW agriculture professor, and Gillespie also wrote a series of articles for the *Laramie Republican-Boomerang* in 1951 and 1952 that were helpful for various sections in this book.

Tom Minor's information came from the personal files of Saratoga historian Elva Evans who graciously provided details, a place to work for a morning of research, and much encouragement. Among her collection was an article about Minor that appeared in *Western Horseman* in 1954. Additional information about Minor's first ride was found in the Dawson Scrapbook at the Colorado History Museum, Denver, Colorado.

The account of Frank Irwin's ride on Steamboat at the 1902 Cheyenne Frontier Days is from the *Wyoming Tribune* and from articles by Burns and Gillespie in the *Laramie Republican-Boomerang*.

CHAPTER THREE

COMPLETE BOOKS HAVE BEEN written about the Swan Land and Cattle Company. Information for our review of that huge operation was collected from "Wyoming Cattle King" by Professor Herbert O. Brayer in the *Western Livestock and Westerner,* (March, 1950), from manuscript notes from Virginia Cole Trenholm for her book, *Footprints on the Frontier: Saga of the LaRamie Region of Wyoming,* and from a manuscript at the Wyoming State Archives composed of various articles copied from 1881 issues of the *Cheyenne Daily Leader* and 1887 issues of the *Northwestern Live Stock Journal.* Other sources were newspaper clippings from the Coe Library Clipping File at the University of Wyoming from the *Wheatland Times,* August 14, 1952 and April 1, 1948; the *Wyoming State Tribune,* December 5, 1943; the *Laramie Daily Boomerang,* December 14, 1943, April 26, 1944, December 3, 1947, and December 19, 1957; the *Chugwater News,* December 11, 1943, and May 4, 1944; the *Kemmerer Gazette,* August 23, 1946; an article, "Stormy ups and downs of the Swan Land and Cattle Company," by Arizola Magnenat, *Platte County Record-Times,* December 16, 1977; an article, "Wyoming Citizen is accepted in Cowboy Hall of Fame," *Gillette News-Record,* July 21, 1960; a historical tour itinerary for the Swan Company Roundup of July 19, 1953; and articles on the M Bar Ranch and Swan Land and Cattle Company in *Platte County Heritage* (Platte County Extension Homemakers Council, 1981).

Anyone wanting more information about W. F. Swan and the Encampment River Swans should consult, *Tough Country, The History of the Saratoga & Encampment Valley, 1825-1895* by Gay Day Alcorn (Legacy Press, 1984). See also *The Swan Land And Cattle Company LTD*, by Harmon Ross Mothershead, (Norman: University of Oklahoma Press, 1971). Other sources were from the manuscript and biographical files of the Grand Encampment Museum, Encampment, Wyoming.

CHAPTER FOUR

TOM HORN IS ONE OF the most well-known historical figures in Wyoming, and his story has been told in a number of books. References for this chapter included *History of Wyoming*, T. A. Larson (Lincoln: University of Nebraska Press, 1965); *The Legend of Tom Horn Last of the Bad Men*, Jay Monaghan (New York City: Bobbs-Merrill, 1946); *The Saga of Tom Horn, The Story of a Cattlemen's War* by Dean F. Krakel (Lincoln: University of Nebraska Press, 1954); *Tom Horn, A Vindication* by Tom Horn (Norman: University of Oklahoma Press, 1904). Much information can be found in the University of Wyoming Clipping File at Coe Library and at the vertical files of both the Wyoming State Archives and Old West Museum. It should be noted that newspapers in Cheyenne in 1903 used different spellings for the name O. M. Eldrich, the merry-go-round engineer involved in the capture of Horn in a 1903 escape attempt.

Information about the Nickell death came from court testimony included in several of the Horn books and from personal interviews conducted by Candy Moulton with Encampment residents Geraldine Ashley Walker and Viola Nickell Bixler about their uncle Willie Nickell. The Nickell family moved from Iron Mountain to Cheyenne after Willie's death, and later settled in the Upper North Platte River Valley, first at Lake Creek north of Saratoga and later at Encampment. Other sources were from 1903 issues of the *Wyoming Tribune*.

For more on Tom Horn see *Tom Horn "Killing Men is My Specialty..."* by Chip Carlson (Cheyenne, Wyoming: Beartooth Corral, 1991).

CHAPTER FIVE

MANY OF THE SAME sources used in Chapter Four were references for the section of this chapter on John Coble. Other material came from the University of Wyoming Clipping File at Coe Library, *Progressive Men of Wyoming* (Chicago: A. W. Bowen and Company, 1903); *Wyoming's Pioneer Ranches,* Robert Burns, A. S. Gillespie, and Willing Richardson (Laramie, Wyoming: Top of the World Press, 1955); an article, "The Cheyenne Club," by Daze M. Bristol, in *Bits and Pieces* (Volume 4, No. 3) in 1968.

Charles B. Irwin's life is well documented in collections at the Wyoming State Archives, Old West Museum, and American Heritage Center. Those voluminous records were used for the portion of this chapter devoted to Irwin. The collections included programs for the Irwin Brothers Wild West Show, numerous obituaries and biographies about Irwin. Other sources were the *Casper Star-Tribune,* March 18, 1978; *Wyoming Tribune,* May 17, 1903, May 31, 1903, August 18, 1906, and August 27, 1910; the *Cheyenne Star,* July 2, 1967; and the *Wyoming Eagle,* June 16 and 18, 1970.

Although we did not use it as a reference, a novel of Irwin's life, *Prairie* by Anna Lee Waldo (Berkley: Charter Books, 1986) tells the fascinating story of Irwin and the Y6 in a fictional format and it lists an extensive bibliography.

CHAPTER SIX

THE COLLECTIONS ON C. B. Irwin, as outlined in Chapter Five citations, were useful in preparing this chapter. Other sources included *The Wild West* by Don Russell located at the Wyoming State Archives; *Westerners Brand Book* (Chicago Posse: Vol. 26, No. 12); the *Wyoming Eagle,* June 16, 1970, and June 18, 1970; and the *Wyoming Tribune,* August 27, 1910. Irwin Brothers programs and general information were found in vertical files at both the Old West Museum and the Wyoming State Archives.

Much of the information for the Buffalo Bill Wild West show and about wild west shows in general came from the McCraken Research Library and files of the Buffalo Bill Historical Center in Cody, Wyoming.

CHAPTER SEVEN

THE STORY OF THE Cheyenne Frontier Days was gathered from newspapers published during that era, including the *Wyoming Tribune*, the *Cheyenne Leader*, and the *Wyoming Semi-Weekly Tribune*. We spent days in Laramie and Cheyenne poring over microfilm copies of all of those papers published about Frontier Days during that era, and then had copies made so we could check and doublecheck our information as we were writing.

The staff of the Wyoming State Archives—Ann Nelson, Jean Brainerd, Rick Ewig, and Roger Joyce—saved us much time and many miles on the road by checking specifics for us as we finalized the manuscript. We truly appreciate their assistance.

While we relied on the newspaper reports for detail in this chapter, a useful reference was *Daddy of 'Em All*, Robert D. Hanesworth (Cheyenne: Flintlock Publishing Co., 1967). It is particularly helpful for having a listing of dates for the celebration annually and a listing of the champions in various events. Also useful was *Cheyenne Frontier Days A Marker From Which to Reckon All Events* by Milt Riske (Cheyenne: Corral of Westerners International and Joy Riske, 1984). Other sources included a manuscript, "Out of the Chutes, Frontier Days in Cheyenne" by Tex Sherman, written for *Ranch Romances*.

Much information was gathered from the vertical files of the Wyoming Archives including, from Folder Number One, a history of Frontier Days from 1897 to 1933. The reminiscences of Ida Gilliand Fox are from an article by Martha Thompson which appeared in the *Cheyenne Eagle*, July 22, 1979. The story of the Mountain and Plain Festival Kuykendall belt is in the *Wyoming Tribune*, July 15, 1903. The information from Warren Richardson, chairman of the first Frontier Days, came from a full page advertisement in the vertical file at the Wyoming Archives entitled, "Frontier Days, The Daddy of 'Em All, Its Beginning;" the ad has no publication information or date. Other sources were "Editor's Suggestion Launched Frontier Days," *Cheyenne Eagle*, February 15, 1976; "4,000 Jam Pioneer Park for First Frontier Show," *Wyoming Eagle*, date unknown; "Frontier is World's Most Famous Rodeo," *Wyoming State Tribune*, July 21, 1942; "Early Bucking Chutes

'Chambers of Horror,'" *Sunday Tribune-Eagle*, Cheyenne, July 21, 1974; "Colorful Star Makes Daddy of 'Em All Tops," *Wyoming Eagle* and *Tribune*, July 25 and 28, 1950. Those articles are located in the vertical file of the State Archives and on microfilm records.

CHAPTER EIGHT

FOR THIS CHAPTER ABOUT Steamboat's demise, we used "Old Steamboat Killed," from the *Cheyenne Daily Leader*, October 15, 1914, and December 13, 1914; "Steamboat Sleeps at Old City Dump," *Wyoming State Tribune*, June 2, 1955 and "That Steamboat Myth," by Fay E. Ward, *Western Horseman*, December, 1966.

CHAPTER NINE

WE FOUND THE HISTORY of the Wyoming license plate printed in *Best Scene, Magazine of the Wyoming State Penitentiary*, and in a separate publication produced by the Saratoga Historical and Cultural Association, Saratoga, Wyoming. We also used "The Beginning of a Great Emblem" by George N. Ostrom which we found at the Wyoming State Archives, a document prepared by the Archives for the Wyoming Centennial and information provided by Wyoming Secretary of State Kathy Karpan in a telephone interview in January 1992. See also references to Guy Holt and Jake Maring. Lester C. Hunt, who put the bucking horse on the Wyoming license plate, was elected governor in 1943 and became Wyoming's U. S. senator in 1948. He was beset by political and personal problems and in June 1954 took his own life.

CHAPTER TEN

WE GATHERED INFORMATION for this chapter from personal interviews conducted by Candy Moulton with Peter M. Fillerup, November 1989, September 1990, and October 1990; and a telephone interview with Greg Taggart, August 1991. We also got information from "The Sculptor" (Vol. 3, No. 1) provided by Peter M. Fillerup; "Steamboat" *Laramie Daily Boomerang*, February 2, 1989. Information also was gathered at the 1990 dedication of *FANNING A TWISTER—STEAMBOAT* at the University of Wyoming Homecoming, October 1990. Portions of this chapter appeared in articles by Candy Moulton in *Southwest Art*, February 1991 and in Wyoming Weekend, *Casper Star-Tribune*, October 10, 1991.

PART TWO

CHAPTER ELEVEN

GATHERING THE INFORMATION for the individual cowboy stories was the biggest challenge of this book, and also the source of our greatest pleasure as we got to know those rugged men who had the skill and guts to climb aboard Steamboat. As previously documented, we compiled our original list of riders from *Steamboat, Symbol of Wyoming Spirit* and newspaper articles in the *Laramie Republican-Boomerang.* The names of other riders were found as we reviewed the sources to find details about those cowboys we knew had climbed on Steamboat. Our search for information about each of the men started at the biography files of the Wyoming State Archives, American Heritage Center, Old West Museum, and at the Coe Library Clipping File. To list every newspaper clipping we reviewed in our search would be a book in itself. Suffice it to say, the files of the following newspapers were used: *Laramie Daily Boomerang, Wyoming State Tribune, Laramie Republican-Boomerang, Wyoming Tribune, Wyoming Semi-Weekly Tribune, Pinedale Roundup, Cheyenne Leader, Saratoga Sun, Denver Post, Sheridan Post, Casper Star-Tribune, Wyoming Eagle, Wheatland Times, Rawlins Daily Times, Cody Enterprise,* and *Billings Gazette.* Our most extensive work centered on the Cheyenne newspapers from the period of 1902 until 1915. Other helpful references were found in *Westerners Brand Book* (Vol. 26, No. 4 and Vol. 26, No. 12) and the Dawson Scrapbook, Colorado State Historical Society, which is located at the Colorado History Museum in Denver, Colorado. Other sources included the *St. Louis Globe Democrat,* October 22, 1900; *New York Herald* April 16, 1905; *Wyoming Rural Electric News,* August 1983; *Wyo Alum News,* February 1952; *Medicine Bow Post,* September 1978; *Annals of Wyoming* (Vol 12, No. 3) and *Bits and Pieces,* July 1965.

In addition to the Cheyenne newspapers of the era specific information for the cowboy stories was obtained as follows:

ART ACORD: The Tex Jordan collection at the American Heritage Center in Laramie was a primary source. Jordan spent years collecting information and writing about Acord. Specific articles were found in the 1974 edition of *Classic Film Collector*; "The 'Reel' West of Art Acord," by Glenn Shirley in the *Westerner*, March-April, 1972; in "About Cowpokes" by Jordan published in *Wild West Stars;* in an article "Art Acord, Jack Hoxie, & Hoot Gibson" in *Ozark Cinema Review*, November, 1975. Information about Acord's involvement with the 101 Ranch Company is from a letter to Jordan dated December 23, 1973, from the Ponca City Rodeo Foundation, Incorporated. Information about Acord's death came from the Jordan files which had a letter from Carlos de Paula Couto, Porto Alegre, Brazil, referring to speculation that Acord died of cyanide poisoning; a note from Johnny Hagner, Palmdale, California, indicating Acord was stabbed to death by a Mexican; and a copy of the Mexican death certificate. Jordan's large collection also includes many letters from and to Harry Webb related to Acord and other topics since both men were western writers.

FRED BATH: We used the autobiographical manuscript, *Musings of a Pioneer* written by Bath and located at the Wyoming State Archives (WPA subject 566). Information also came from *Wyoming's Pioneer Ranches*, cited earlier, and "Fred Bath Dies in Denver After Notable Career," in the *Laramie Republican-Boomerang*, September 26, 1931.

HARRY BRENNAN: We used the *Wyoming Tribune*, September 2, 1904, and September 21, 1904; *Sheridan County Directories*, 1907 and 1908; *Horse Wrangler* by Floyd C. Bard (Norman: University of Oklahoma Press, 1960) and biographical files at the National Cowboy Hall of Fame and Western Heritage Center in Oklahoma City, Oklahoma.

AL CATON: Information came from "Broncho Busting Great Feature," *Laramie Boomerang*, September 15, 1905 and articles written by Burns and Gillespie.

HUGH CLARK: We used "Clark, Donald and Jane" *Platte County Heritage* (Wheatland, Wyoming: Platte County Extension Homemakers Council, 1981); *Cheyenne Leader*, August 27 and 28, 1903, and Burns and Gillespie.

MORRIS CORTHELL: Information is from the Corthell Collection, American Heritage Center, Laramie, Wyoming; a personal letter to the authors from Amy King, Corthell's daughter, and articles by Burns and Gillespie.

WILLIAM CRAVER: We used the *Wyoming Tribune*, August 15, 1906, and August 15, 1966; the *New York Herald*, April 16, 1905; Burns and Gillespie's writings and the Dawson Scrapbook.

CLAYTON DANKS: Information came from "King of the Hurricane Deck" by Clayton Danks as told to 'Tana Mac, *Frontier Times*, Spring 1962; "Two Wyoming Champions" by Art Fee, *Wyoming Rural Electric News*, August 1983; "Fremont County Man Once Champ Bronc Buster," *Northern Wyoming Daily News*, Worland, July 9, 1949; "Danks, Champion Bronc Rider and Lawman, Dies," *Rawlins Daily Times*, July 11, 1965; *Wyoming State Tribune*, June 25, 1970; *Wyoming Eagle*, June 26, 1972; *Casper Star-Tribune*, June 25, 1970; *Denver Post*, October 20, 1960; *Wyoming State Journal*, July 5, 1962. Information also came from the biographical files of National Cowboy Hall of Fame and Western Heritage Center and the Dawson Scrapbook.

JIMMY DANKS: Biographical files of the Wyoming State Archives were used. Also see references to Chapter Two.

FRED DODGE: Much of the information was provided by Dodge's granddaughter, Sherry McKay, who was working as a typesetter at the *Saratoga Sun* when she spotted an item about plans for this book. She had a collection of clippings, letters, a contract Dodge signed for one of his stints with the Buffalo Bill Wild West Show, photographs, and other personal papers. Another source was an article about Dodge by his daughter, Doris Ledbetter, in the Wyoming Centennial book, *Saratoga & Encampment Wyoming An Album of Family Histories* (The Woodlands, Texas: Portfolio Publishing Co., 1989).

PAUL HANSEN: Information came from references in newspapers and other writings of Burns and Gillespie. We particularly used a letter written by Hansen to Gillespie in 1952.

MIKE HASTINGS: We gathered details from the biographical files at the National Cowboy Hall of Fame and Western Heritage Center and from Burns and Gillespie information.

GUY HOLT: Much of the information came from family records including correspondence and clippings kept by Gwen Holt Woodward, Guy's eldest daughter. Mrs. Woodward spent much time and effort in 1975 and 1976 trying to get the Denver Festival of Mountain and Plain belt, won by Thad Sowder in 1901 and 1902 and by Guy Holt in 1903, donated to the National Cowboy Hall of Fame in Oklahoma City, Oklahoma. The belt, which had to be won by the same cowboy three times before it could be kept, was only contested three times. It is now located at the Denver History Museum in the Kuykendall Collection where it has been since 1935 when Mrs. John Kuykendall donated it to the State Historical Society of Colorado. Other information came from personal interviews with Evelyn Infanger, Florence Lozier, Tom Holt, and Ethel Smith about their father Guy Holt; a tape recording by Ethel Smith; a Rodeo Sports News publication *Wild Bunch*, December, 1975; an article "Back of the Chutes," by Gene Lamb, in *The Horse Lover's Magazine*, July-August, 1967; a letter of introduction from the editor of the *Wyoming Daily Tribune* and *Semi-Weekly Tribune* for Guy Holt to attend the St. Louis Exposition in 1905 as a winner of the *Wyoming Tribune's* Most Popular Cowboy Contest from Flossie Moulton's personal collection about her grandfather. Other sources were "Guy Holt is declared Champion Rough Rider," *The Denver Post*, August 28, 1903; "Holt and Wines are the Champion Broncho Busters of the World," the *Denver Post*, August 30, 1903; "Champion Holt Dethroned," *Laramie Boomerang*, September 24, 1903; "Great Fair Closes in a Blaze of Glory," *Laramie Boomerang*, September, 25, 1903; letter from Annie Holt to the *Wyoming State Tribune*, in 1946; "T. D. Holt passed away at home near Cora Thurs." *Pinedale Roundup*, April 2, 1931; "Guy Holt died at Jackson Hospital" *Pinedale Roundup*, June 27, 1946.

FRANK IRWIN: *Cheyenne Leader*, August 27, 1902, August 28, 1902, and August 19, 1902, provided information. We also gathered general information from the Irwin collection at the Wyoming State Archives and from Burns and Gillespie.

JAKE MARING: We used the *Laramie Republican Boomerang*, August 13, 1954; information provided by Laramie resident Emery Miller; and material from Burns and Gillespie.

EDDIE MCCARTY: Our sources included the biographical files provided by the National Cowboy Hall of Fame and Western Heritage Center and writings by Burns and Gillespie.

CHARLES MCKINLEY: We used the *Wyoming Tribune*, August 19, 1912, and writings by Burns and Gillespie.

TOM MINOR: Information was located in the personal files of Elva Evans of Saratoga, Wyoming, including an article in *Western Horseman*, May 1977. We also located information in the Dawson Scrapbook and used references from Burns and Gillespie.

KID MOORE: We used an Irwin Brothers Wild West Show Program, located in the Irwin vertical file of the Old West Museum.

WILLIAM MURRAY: Information came from the *Wyoming Tribune* August 17, 1906, from "Early 1900s Frontier Days Cowboy Remembers" in the *Wyoming Eagle*, Cheyenne, November 28, 1974, and from Burns and Gillespie.

CRAVEL PAGUS: We used information from the files of the Buffalo Bill Historical Center, Cody, Wyoming.

OTTO PLAGA: Much of the information came from personal files of Elva Evans in Saratoga, Wyoming, and from a WPA file provided by the Wyoming State Archives. We also used articles in the *Saratoga Sun,* dated January 21, 1931 and July 4, 1990. Thelma Plaga Garton answered questions about her uncle, Otto Plaga, in a telephone interview in June of 1991, and she provided us with the original typewritten copy of biographical information prepared at the time of Plaga's death. We also used the previously cited *Platte County Heritage* and *Footprints on the Frontier: Saga of the Laramie Region of Wyoming* by Virginia Cole Trenholm (Douglas, Wyoming: Douglas Enterprise, 1945) and various works about the Tom Horn trial as cited in chapter four.

THAD SOWDER: We used "Polly Pry talks with 'Thad,' the Champion Rough Rider," *The Denver Post*, October 6, 1901; "Sowders and Peggy are a Pair Very Hard to Beat," *The Denver Post,* October 4, 1901; "Thad Sowder again wins honors in exciting Broncho Busting Contest," *The Daily News* (Denver), August 2, 1903; "Bronc Busting introduced," *Rocky Mountain News*, May 4, 1952, and issues of the *Saratoga Sun* from March 19, 1931, July 18, 1907, and June 24, 1982. Information also was provided from the personal files of Saratoga historian and author Gay Day Alcorn who was a great inspiration to the authors. Other newspaper sources included the *Wyoming Tribune*, June 6, 1903, July 30, 1903; August 2, 1903, and September 7, 1903.

DICK STANLEY: Our outlaw cowboy was great fun to research. We used "Stanley and Steamboat," by Milt C. Riske in *Old Timers Wild West*, April 1979; Hanesworth's, *Daddy of 'Em All*, cited earlier; an untitled manuscript in the Cheyenne Frontier Days vertical file at the Wyoming State Archives; and a manuscript, "A Rangeland Renegade," by J. Elmer Brock, which was located at the American Heritage Center in Laramie and useful for the information it contained about Stanley's early days in Wyoming. We also found information about Stanley at the Denver History Museum and in the Dawson Scrapbook located there.

FRANK STONE: Sources in addition to the newspapers of Steamboat's era included "B. Frank Stone Famed as Rider of Old Steamboat," the *Laramie Republican*, September, 14, 1944; and "Stone's Case is Dismissed," *Laramie Boomerang*, September 26, 1903.

BILL TAPPAN: We used an article in the previously cited *Saratoga & Encampment Wyoming An Album of Family Histories* and received other information from Betty Merrill of Encampment, Wyoming.

HARRY WEBB: Much information about Webb was found in a collection under his name, a biographical file, and in the Tex Jordan Collection all at the American Heritage Center in Laramie. Information also was located at the Buffalo Bill Historical Center in Cody, Wyoming. Specific articles used included "Pine Mountain Storyteller," *Nevada Magazine*, date unknown, and "Bronc Rider for Buffalo Bill" by Loren Ledin in *True West*, June 1982. Both of those articles were found at the Buffalo Bill Historical Center. Items from the Webb Collection at the American Heritage Center included "First Place Award," *Westerner*, Summer 1973; and the following articles written by Webb: "Call of the Cow Country,"

Westerner, July-August, 1972; "Harry Webb's Cow Country," *Westerner,* September-October, 1972; "The Youngest Bronc-Buster in Wyoming," *Westerner,* January-February, 1973; "I Remember Those Good Old Days," *Westerner,* March-April, 1973; "My Years with Buffalo Bill's Wild West Show, Part 1, and Part 2 in *Real West,* Fall issues, 1974; "Tenderfoot Cowboy," in *The West,* date unknown; "My Days as an Old-Time Movie Cowboy," *Westerner,* Fall, 1975; "The Satan Horse," *Westerner,* March-April, 1974; "Hey Rube!" by Edgar Webb, (Harry's pseudonym), *Westerner,* Spring, 1976; and "Old 'Wild West' Star Can't Stand Tinsel Cowboys, the *Denver Post,* February 7, 1982. Other sources were the *Westerner,* February, 1971 and April, 1971.

INDEX

183

ABOUT THE AUTHORS

BOTH FLOSSIE MOULTON AND Candy Moulton are third generation Wyoming natives.

Flossie was born near Jackson where she ranched with her husband, Harley, on land that is now a part of Grand Teton National Park. For the past 30-years she has lived near Cody, Wyoming. She has five children and seven grandchildren.

Her writing has appeared in newspapers and agricultural magazines. This book was inspired by her longstanding interest in the bucking horse, Steamboat, and as a memorial to her grandfather, Guy Holt.

Candy has lived her entire life near Encampment, Wyoming, except for the years she attended college. Her writing and photography have appeared in *Southwest Art, True West, Time*, the *Chicago Tribune,* and many other national publications, as well as in Wyoming newspapers and magazines.

She was inspired to make her living as a writer by her high school English teacher, Grace Healey, and her first newspaper editor/publisher, Dick Perue. They taught her grammar and the importance of deadlines.

*This book was printed on
55-pound Huron
acid-free, recycled paper.*